Talking to Learn

Talking to Learn

Classroom Practices in Teaching English,
Vol. 24

Patricia Phelan, Chair,
and the Committee on Classroom Practices

National Council of Teachers of English
1111 Kenyon Road, Urbana, Illinois 61801

NCTE Editorial Board: Donald R. Gallo, Richard Lloyd-Jones, Raymond Rodrigues, Dorothy Strickland, Brooke Workman; Charles Suhor, ex officio; Michael Spooner, ex officio

Book Design: Tom Kovacs for TGK Design

Staff Editor: Tim Bryant

NCTE Stock Number 50020-3020

Library of Congress Catalog Card Number 85-644740

Contents

Preface

Our 1987–88 Committee on Classroom Practices chose to issue a call for manuscripts which would promote students' speaking and listening abilities. We were specifically interested in successful classroom practices which used oral communication to develop student confidence in a variety of speaking situations and to expand student understanding of literature through both analysis and performance. The committee viewed talking and listening as everyday classroom experiences which lead to increased learning through better reading comprehension and improved written expression of ideas.

After our November 1987 meeting, the call for manuscripts was issued in *Language Arts, English Journal, Council-Grams, College English,* and *English Education,* as well as in the journals of NCTE-affiliated organizations. By September of 1988, we had received many manuscripts from teachers throughout the country. These manuscripts, with authors' names removed, were evaluated by committee members Carlota Cárdenas de Dwyer, Beverly Busching, Nancy Broz, Kent Gill, Jackie Proett, and Iris McClellan Tiedt—a committee representing several geographic areas and grade levels.

Twenty-four manuscripts were finally selected and submitted to the NCTE Editorial Board for approval to publish. All of the contributions represent exemplary classroom practices using talking and listening activities to further learning. The committee hopes this volume will provide new ideas to help teachers extend student learning in their own classrooms.

Introduction

In the classroom we use talking and listening activities to help students develop self-confidence, to help them expand their understanding of literature, and to help them clarify their ideas in both spoken and written expression. Included here you will find practices to help you create in your own classroom an environment in which students share ideas, listen to one another, respect each other's similarities and differences, and really care about learning. Teachers from elementary, middle school, secondary, and college levels have contributed to this volume successful classroom practices using talking and listening to enhance learning.

You will be able to take the ideas presented here and adapt them to your own grade level, modifying the strategies and materials to suit your students. For example, Norton's article on teaching personification and Kempthorne's presentation on point of view are easily adaptable to any grade level, depending on the sophistication of the literature you choose. Johnson's chapter on strategies for developing effective use of the voice is intended for an elementary-level audience but would be equally effective in a secondary classroom. Henderson's panel presentations can be adapted to most grade levels by adjusting the level of difficulty of the ideas used.

The first section of this volume is composed of activities using talking and listening to expand students' understanding of literature. Underhill shows you one way to get started so that students will listen to each other as they discuss. Three creative uses of a tape recorder to collect student responses and reading of poetry follow. Responses to literature include a talk show format, small-group collaboration, sharing of reading response journals, and talking about and performing literature and plays, as well as a speaking project about the arts which connects the students' real world with the classroom.

The second section is composed of talking and listening activities designed to develop students' self-confidence in speaking before a group and listening effectively. Johnson shows students how to use their voices effectively. Hardin offers activities combining persuasive

1

writing and speaking. Thanos and Avadian show students how to "map" a speech for a formal presentation. Suggestions for a classroom debate and panel presentations based on student research follow. Wallace offers ways of improving communication across cultures in an international business class. Wyatt explains how finding the underlying pattern in a speech aids student confidence in listening. Ways to weave listening and speaking throughout the school day follow in Plourde's essay. This section also includes two different approaches to an interview: Thomas aims at student interviews based on controversial topics, while DeZure shows students how to be sensitive to the beauty in other people's lives—to learn to hear the message *behind* the words they say. Cassells' talking to close the school year with a positive touch concludes on just the right note.

Throughout this volume you will find talking and listening activities used as ways into writing, from essays to research reports. Reading the writing aloud, talking about the ideas, and listening to suggestions, in small groups or pairs, are often mentioned. Talking and listening in response to literature, prior to writing a formal response, is also common in a number of chapters. The writers in this volume share a common understanding that talking and listening activities promote learning through promoting clarity of thinking and expression. We believe these classroom practices will provide successful learning experiences for you and your students.

Patricia Phelan, Chair
Committee on Classroom Practices in Teaching English

I Talking to Expand Understanding of Literature

1 Follow the Bouncing Ball

Harlan Underhill
Greenhills School
Ann Arbor, Michigan

The ninth graders were bouncing off the wall. Well, not quite literally, but close. My new student teacher, Leslie, was conducting one of her first discussions. I had retired to the tablet armchair at the back of the room. About half of the students were engaged in yelling across the room at each other remarks such as "Achilles was STUPID to go back into battle!" or "YOU DUMMY! He HAD to! It was his FATE!" The rest were engaged in private conversations of a similar nature or commenting snidely to each other about the people who were shouting. In particular, the little blond twelve-year-old who was taking calculus that year was standing at his place successfully out-arguing those across the room, making up in logical power and command of the reading what he lacked in height. I wasn't worried about Leslie; she had already proved herself a tough and astute classroom manager. I was, however, somewhat embarrassed for myself. Here I was, a teacher of many years' experience who had already had these kids for a semester and had not yet managed to "accustom them to productive discussion."

Leslie stood up, sat on the desk, and swung her feet over into the hollow square of tables. That got their attention. After taking in good humor their remarks on her small silver plastic lizard-skin loafers, she said, "This can't go on. We have to find a way to have an orderly discussion. Only *one* person can talk at a time and the rest *have* to listen. You guys are as noisy as the Greeks on the beach. Any suggestions about how to do it?"

"Way to go, Leslie," I thought.

The silence was only momentary. First came the standard adolescent appeals to authority:

"YOU call on us."

"Throw anyone who talks out of class."

Then, the dour dark-haired comic book freak said, "I'll bring in a pole and make a scepter. Then we can pass it around, just like in the Achaean assemblies."

"I've got an even better idea," yelled the twelve-year-old calculus student, jumping out of his chair and zipping toward the door as the bell rang. "I've got a nerf soccer ball. I'll bring it in tomorrow."

As the room emptied I turned to Leslie and we both said, "A nerf soccer ball?"

The next day the diminutive genius did in fact bring in a light sponge-rubber ball about the size of a grapefruit painted with the black and white pentagons of a soccer ball. Instead of merely calling on someone, Leslie threw the ball to a student with a hand up. He or she spoke until they were finished and then tossed the ball to someone else with a hand up or back to Leslie.

They were charmed by the new game. Only one of the boys winged it at someone else, and surprisingly the act met with a murmur of disapproval and was not repeated. One of the girls caught awkwardly, but most were in sports and were ready to enter in. The girls tried extra-hard because for once they saw the chance of getting their say without being shouted down by thickening vocal cords.

After three or so days in which the procedure worked fairly well, the students began to be impatient with the time lost in actually throwing the ball back and forth. We switched to merely having the student who was talking call on the next speaker from among those with raised hands. I kept a tally on the board by initials so that everyone could see how many times someone had spoken. The students' instinctive fairness limited the loudmouths somewhat; in addition, Leslie kept urging them quietly to pick someone who hadn't spoken yet.

No game works forever, though. As the early warm weather of spring arrived, our resolution to insist on truly courteous discussion diminished. Nor did we ever get to the final stage of a discussion in which students participated spontaneously yet decorously, one by one, without the cues of either the nerf ball or a raised hand. The closest we came was on that day late in the spring on which the county communicable diseases physician had spoken to an assembly on AIDS. The students responded to the additional opportunity we afforded them to discuss the disease in class by doing so with model respect for each others' opinions. Whether it was the topic itself that drew forth such behavior or whether the prior practice had helped, I cannot say, but at least it demonstrated that the kind of discussion we had been aiming at was at least possible for students of that age.

The decorous give-and-take of those intense yet serious discussions on the choices facing Achilles and on the choices the students themselves faced in their own lives was among the most satisfying classroom time I spent last year. A number of years before I had used a variant in the tenth grade with success: I picked the first speaker of the hour. Then, that speaker having finished, I picked the next from among those with raised hands. I stipulated that there could be no repeat speakers until everyone had had a chance, and I kept a tally on a scrap of paper. They immediately introduced a wrinkle that would permit a dialogue between two particularly engaged speakers; that device was the "yield," in which someone who had not yet spoken yielded to a previous speaker who wanted to reply to a point.

I now use a similar procedure in the eighth grade for reading original compositions out loud: I pick the first reader, and then that student, having read, chooses the next. I stipulate that boys must choose girls and girls boys. I continue to be bothered both by the fact that some are consistently not chosen until late in the hour and by the faint traces of party-game romance that these rules introduce. Nevertheless, methods by which a speaking student determines when he or she will relinquish the floor rather than the teacher's functioning as chairman have worked successfully at least for limited periods of time at three grade levels. The nerf-ball method provides a vivid physical analogue of the kind of courteous, decorous, yet spontaneous discussion we probably all hold as essential to real exploration and examination of a topic. In particular, I enjoyed seeing the students participating in finding the means to what I suspect were their own real ends—getting themselves heard by their peers.

Perhaps some year, I'll give an extra-credit assignment in which students are invited to research and construct a proper scepter for an assembly of the Homeric heroes. We'll elect a Talthybios or Eurybates and see whether that physical analogue of the good discussion procedure I'd like them to internalize is any more effective or less hokey than our experiments in 1987 with following the bouncing nerf ball.

2 "You See Their Interselves": Small-Group Discussion of Poetry

Louann Reid
Douglas County High School
Castle Rock, Colorado

In teaching poetry, most of us have encountered secondary students who feel exactly like the following second grader, although they may express it differently: "Poetry is icky. I wish poetry was out of sight. I wish it were out of this world, or at least in Europe" (Harp, as quoted in Pattison 1975, p. 15). Most students and many teachers view poetry as something studied in school, then best forgotten. Students find the language, ideas, and sentence structure difficult, and teachers find too few resources available to help them solve students' difficulties.

I first became interested in a new method of improving speaking, listening, and response to poetry in the summer of 1984 when I heard Peter Benton of Oxford, England, discuss his work with groups of thirteen-year-olds discussing poems without a teacher. I decided to study the students in my classes to see if they were as capable as the British students Benton described. Later I attended a workshop by Canadian professor Patrick Dias, who helped me further refine Benton's procedures to fit my students. I now use the following steps:

1. Ask students to read the poem at least once before class to develop questions or a possible interpretation.

2. On the day of the discussion, have students form groups of three to five. Give each group a tape recorder and the following instructions:

   "Talk about the poem until you have nothing else you want to say about it. If you quit and then return to it, please indicate that on the tape. You may want to consider the following four questions, although you don't have to: (1) What is the poem about? (2) How does it say what it is saying? (3) What do you like or dislike about it? (4) Why do you feel the way you do?"

3. After twenty or thirty minutes, have one person from each group report to the whole class. After each group has reported, all students may discuss the differences in interpretations. You may also want to ask for clarification of vague or unsupported statements and provide closure by summarizing the interpretations.

The following excerpt from a discussion about the poem "Boar's Head," by Georgia poet Tom Liner (reprinted at the end of this chapter), shows that students are capable of carrying on this sort of discussion. Although only two of them speak in the following section of the tape, four boys are discussing this poem, which is about a trophy hanging over the mantel. Although the boar's eyes are usually dull and "it hangs there / gross and tasteless like a bad joke," the head changes in the firelight. The speaker implies his feelings as he remembers the boar's life and the moment of the kill with "the hounds dying / in the mingled blood of beast and beast."

> *1*: What I want to know is why did he call it "Boar's Head?" I mean, I know why he called it that, but why did he write about such a stupid thing?
>
> *2*: 'Cause it makes you think about things. You know, it makes you think about hunting, where you go out to kill it just to put it on your mantelpiece.
>
> *1*: That's disgusting.
>
> [They discuss the meaning of *taxidermist* and where boars live.]
>
> *1*: Why would he write about killing something and then it comes back to life? Is that what it says? Because he kills it, then it's on his mantelpiece, then [interrupted by next speaker]
>
> *2*: When he looks in his eyes that's what he gets from the feeling of it. . . . But that's . . . I mean when you look into something's eyes, you get a feeling of something different, don't you?
>
> *1*: Yeah, that sort of changes the whole plot of the story.
>
> *2*: But seriously, when you look into someone's eyes you see . . .
>
> *1*: You see . . .
>
> *2*: You see what they . . .
>
> *1*: You see their interself.
>
> *2*: But seriously, when you look into somebody's eyes, you see what they feel, what they see, and how they see it, in somebody else's eyes.

These boys have worked their way through the poem, using evidence from it and from their background knowledge. They return to the first boy's question about the subject of the poem until he is satisfied that they have answered it. He realizes that the poet is talking about understanding the feelings of others (their "interself"), and the second boy summarizes that section of the discussion.

In a whole-class discussion, the progress is often linear, moving from recall to comprehension to analysis and evaluation. There is seldom time to loop back to previous questions. In addition, it is impossible for any teacher to know what each student does not know, and it is intimidating for students to ask. Yet they are capable of much more than we might imagine. I have found evidence in several discussions that most questions can be answered by the group members. Someone always seems to know what a taxidermist is or where boars live, for example. Students also get around to asking the same sort of questions a teacher would, but because they raise issues of theme or language when those issues are relevant to them, they will remember longer the meaning they have constructed.

Unfortunately, successful small-group discussions do not just happen. Oh, we all know the advantages of group discussion: students talk more when the intimidation of the large group is absent, they listen to each other instead of tuning out the teacher, and they collaborate to construct the meaning of the work. However, the disadvantages are equally obvious. There is nothing more discouraging (or noisy) than a group or groups who are off the task. Do not assume that just putting students in groups will bring about meaningful discussions. We must prepare them for a form of instruction that may be unfamiliar. Devote at least two class periods early in the term for students to get to know each other (excellent suggestions are in Gere 1985). Then, be sure that the task and your expectations for the end product, such as reporting back or individual written interpretations, are clear.

Let students know that you care about their success. Make sure they know you think the discussion is serious business. That does not mean hovering over them as they work, but it does mean being available if they have questions and occasionally walking around from group to group.

The best device I've found to convey this message is the tape recorder. After some initial recorder shyness, students seem to ignore the machine as they discuss the poem. Putting a tape recorder in every group serves three purposes. First, when students know you plan to listen to the discussion, they take it seriously and stay on task. Second, when you listen to the tapes, you learn so much more about individual students than you could through whole-class discussion alone. It is an ideal way to analyze students' speaking, listening, and response skills. Finally, it is useful to have students listen to the tape on another day and analyze their own skills. Research tells us that metacognition—thinking about thinking—leads to increased learning (Jones 1985, Reeve and Brown 1984, Vygotsky 1978).

Through this process of active speaking and listening, students can learn more without enjoying it less. They become confident that they can "figure out" a poem without having to resort to an outside authority. An added benefit of this method for teachers is that, like the boy discussing "Boar's Head," we realize that we can see the students' inner selves as we listen to what *they* have to say.

BOAR'S HEAD
by Tom Liner
(reprinted by permission of the author)

the light has gone out of its eyes
now dull glass
done by the taxidermist's unholy hands
eyes tamed and dead, blind

it hangs there
gross and tasteless like a bad joke
an ugly decoration for the mantel

no breath there
tusks blunted and dry

but when the wind is cold
and the fire smothers red ashes

sometimes it changes

the shadows move in the corners
and the glass eyes shine
they take and hold the light
drawing fire in
they grow liquid and glare
rage

as they did once in the hot woods
glaring at the sun
absorbing its white heat
from the insect-droning air
heat feeding hot blood
of a heart made to kill

the snout moistens
sniffs the scent of hounds
and coarse hair bristles twitch
ears flick and quiver scarred
by death-fights in the gloom
of pine-thicket and black-water swamp
hearing the hounds of its death coming
howling in the shadow-trembling woods

tusks grow sharp again
silvered with saliva
and its breath is foul and hot
with the hunger to slash and stab
to rage among the baying dogs
in a fierce and dusty tangle
of fangs and ripped bellies
to kill until the fire goes out of its eyes
and to die, killing

I sit on the hearth beside the dying fire
remembering the day in the hot woods
remembering the hounds dying
in the mingled blood of beast and beast

I look at the dead glass eyes holding light
and its breath burns, burns in my mouth.

References

Gere, A. R. 1985. *Roots in the Sawdust: Writing to Learn across the Disciplines.* Urbana, Ill.: NCTE.

Harp, M. W. 1972. Poetry in the Primary Grades. *Elementary English* 49: 1172. Quoted in S. D. Pattison, "What is Poetry? Who Cares?" In *Reading as a Thinking Process: Proceedings of the Annual Reading Conference* (June 12–13, 1975), p. 15.

Jones, B. F. 1985. *Student Cognitive Processing of Text-Based Instruction: An Interaction of the Reader, the Text, and the Teacher.* Paper presented at the annual meeting of the American Educational Research Association, Chicago.

Reeve, R. A., and A. L. Brown. 1984. *Metacognition Reconsidered: Implications for Intervention Research.* Technical Report No. 328. Champaign, Ill.: Center for the Study of Reading, University of Illinois.

Vygotsky, L. S. 1978. *Mind in Society: The Development of Higher Psychological Processes.* Cambridge, Mass.: Harvard University Press.

3 Learning Poetic Mood through the Fine Arts

Elizabeth Altenburger
St. Agnes Academy
Houston, Texas

The most exciting lessons I've ever taught were in the poetry unit. Yes! The neglected—"I'll get around to it"—unit. If the classroom teacher can hook into something familiar for the students, then he or she has captured the spirit necessary to lead to critical analysis of a literary piece, specifically poetry. Poetic mood is one element of poetry that students understand in other forms, for example, in music. Therefore, drawing upon familiar music would be a good beginning.

For this activity, it is best to divide the class into approximately four groups, with the teacher serving as a fifth response unit. Tape recorders are needed for each group. Ask for a volunteer from each group to bring any musical tape the following day while a different volunteer brings any picture (from a magazine or book), art print (check with the art teacher), or painting (from home or the public library). The teacher should also bring a tape and a picture, plus a copy of a poem for each individual in the class.

The activity begins with listening. Each response group listens to another group's tape, with the teacher accepting a student tape and one group accepting the teacher's tape. (If the students "jam" to the music, it's OK! Just be sure you're in control.) After listening a short while, the students and the teacher respond in writing to one of the following questions: "How does this make you feel?" "What mood does this put you in?" Responses will vary greatly from "happy" to "sad" to a possible teacher's response of "frantic" to Heart or Sammy Hagar. These written individual feelings are shared by each member of the group within the small-group setting. One student volunteer records the consensus of the group before they listen to the teacher's next question: "What is there in the music that produces this feeling in you?" Individuals respond in writing and share with the group.

The recorder writes the group consensus. Encourage a different group member to read the group response this time, after playing a short portion of the tape for the rest of the class. Responses to the music may touch on rhythm, vocabulary, beat, or subject matter. When the teacher presents, it is important to suggest that we each bring certain factors to bear on any piece of art, whether music, poetry, or the visual arts. These factors include age, background, exposure to the form, and maturity. Request student volunteers to verbally elaborate on this suggestion. As the students see the other class members and the teacher willingly presenting and discussing without arguing, their fear of the speaking mode should begin to diminish.

Next, circulate the picture, print, or painting to another group and ask each individual to write his or her response to the following question: "What emotion does this picture elicit?" The group should select a new recorder who notes the group consensus. Next question: "What devices does the artist use to create that emotion for you?" Responses may include the colors, the texture, the subject matter, or whether people are in it or not. The emotions may be fear, anger, love, or nostalgia. Encourage a different group member to share the group response with the class. Another group may comment on the finding, and variations in suggested moods should be explored verbally. As long as a student can explain or support his or her reasoning, the answer is OK.

Remember that the teacher's age may have a decisive bearing upon his or her response to a popular musical piece or to pop art or to any form, whereas the students may find the teacher's selections old-fashioned. Nevertheless, the reasons will work into the proper vocabulary of mood. The students and teacher bring background, family, socioeconomic conditions—basically all that they are—to the arts. So does each artist.

A single poem should be read at this point, first silently and individually, and then in unison. (You might try Robert Browning's "Pippa's Song" or Shelley's "A Lament.") A choral reading of this nature frees the shy student to verbalize. Choral reading may be a new experience for most students, and they may be surprised to realize that although they spoke the same words, they could hear others ahead or behind in the reading. They may have heard different inflections or tone of voice, also. Comment on this, but let it serve for another day's elaborative lesson. The written response to the reading should answer the following questions: "What mood is expressed?" "What words, lines, rhythm, or subject matter led you to identify this mood?" "What difference is there between your feelings after each reading?" These responses should be shared with the whole group. Hopefully, by this time, introverted students will volunteer to read their responses. There are no wrong answers, if the student can support his or her findings. The teacher should not have a preconceived answer. To prove your position of fairness, ask the students to bring in poetry which you, the teacher, can read and comment upon sight unseen.

Following this one- to two-day exercise, have students bring in complementary pieces of art, music, and poetry to share orally with the class. Their presentations or monologues should invite discussion of mood. If space is available, the teacher could provide a triptych over which the student drapes a piece of fabric, the color of which complements the mood being created. The print or picture is attached, or a copy of the poem is framed with something as simple as construction paper and is placed near the backdrop or on a small easel. A three-dimensional object might add to the overall picture. The tape could be played and the poem read before the discussion of mood. This last suggestion should be modeled first by the teacher.

This small lesson for a poetry unit could be extended to include listening for tone of voice, for audience, and perhaps for purpose, as well as extended to a discussion of the literary devices. Present these in forms familiar to the students and build from these specifics to the whole poem. By building from specific to general, we lead the student to deeper critical thinking (synthesis) instead of the usual method of presenting the whole poem and tearing it apart into its components (analysis). If the poetry unit is designed to culminate in original writing by the student, then the teacher must give the keys to designing a poem before that student would know where to begin. The use of other fine arts as teaching tools lends itself to the poetry unit.

Listening and speaking skills are only two of the four skills needed for the interactive classroom encouraged by James Moffett and by Louise Rosenblatt. The other two skills, reading and writing, are usually attended to, but listening and learning, as well as risking to speak, must be strengthened. Short, nonthreatening responses will lead to less student fear. Action by other classmates reduces the "on-stage" feeling, also. Finally, writing first before speaking gives the student security. Security, ultimately, leads to more participation. And the more interaction between students, the better the lesson!

References

Moffett, James. 1968. *Teaching the Universe of Discourse.* Boston, Mass.: Houghton Mifflin.

Rosenblatt, Louise M. 1978. *The Reader, the Text, the Poem.* Carbondale, Ill.: Southern Illinois University Press.

4 From Boom Box to Pegasus

Ann R. Morris
Stetson University

Robert Frost remarks in one of his best-known essays that a poem "begins in delight and ends in wisdom." Although most of us would certainly agree, those who have ever taught a unit on poetry also know the frustration of trying to transmit this enthusiasm to students, who generally value a poem about as much as they would cherish a refrigerator in an igloo. In an attempt to overcome this general antipathy for poetry and to persuade students to pat Pegasus's nose even if they won't mount and ride, I have tried everything from introducing the poetry unit with selected lyrics from Simon and Garfunkel to dramatizing Matthew Arnold's "Dover Beach" with darkened room and a recording of waves washing down the dreary shingles of the world. Most of the time the class has sat there, unmoved, more like cow patties in the meadow than riders of the skies. However, one of my most successful attempts to generate excitement about poetry involves a listening-and-speaking exercise that challenges students to use their boom boxes for something other than the latest rock music.

I begin this assignment by playing a twenty-six-minute tape of Gilbert Highet's "The Sounds of Poetry," recorded in 1968 but still timely and readily available (Jeffrey Norton Publishers, 145 E. 49th St., New York, NY 10017). I ask the class to take notes on this tape and in the remainder of the class period to write a summary of and short reaction to Highet's comments. The renowned Oxford don's lecture is easy to follow; in his clipped English accent he analyzes how sounds and rhythms are used by poets. Making the point that most poetry was written to be spoken, sung, or chanted, he emphasizes that readers are likely to miss "the pleasure of the ear." He then discusses what rhyme, alliteration, and rhythm contribute to poetry, interlacing his comments with examples ranging from W. S. Gilbert's *The Pirates of Penzance* to Milton's *Paradise Lost.* He even quotes briefly from French, Italian, and German poems, lines not all of which will be understood by our students—nor even by most of us—but demonstrating how sounds can convey an emotional impression even if content is not understood.

Throughout his lecture Highet avoids technical terms as much as possible. For example, he does not mention assonance and consonance but focuses on alliteration, demonstrating how the sibilant *s* can convey horror and how the quiet, breathy *f* can suggest the soft activities of springtime. Similarly, Highet does not complicate meter by naming numerous types of feet but speaks only of iambic pentameter's "heroic line" before showing how poets use repetition with variation of alternating stressed and unstressed syllables, thus creating rhythm which satisfies an innate desire in humans. Obviously Highet's approach is designed to develop appreciation of poetry rather than ability to scan lines.

Once the students have listened to the taped lecture and written a response to it, I ask them to make tapes of their own. Specifically, their assignment is to choose any poem they want (sometimes I limit their choice to the textbook we are using in the course) and to prepare a six- to eight-minute speech during which they (1) introduce the poem, explaining briefly what it is about; (2) read the entire poem aloud; and (3) demonstrate how the sounds of the poem create particular moods and attitudes. Instead of presenting comments directly to the class, each student prepares a tape. I suggest that they can cut expenses by sharing a tape, but each student must work independently. They are cautioned not to focus too much recording time on reading the poem but rather to choose appropriate phrases and lines from the poem to support their analysis and whatever generalizations they make. I usually try to arrange a "recording studio" where students can work. I make available the Highet tape if students wish to listen to it again, and I always provide a tape recorder for any students who don't have access to one.

After the students' taped lectures have been turned in and I have responded to them—usually on the tape rather than in writing—I play a few of the best in a class and invite comments, thus providing another listening-speaking experience.

The results of this assignment have been gratifying. In listening to and commenting on Gilbert Highet's lecture, students get practice in note-taking and in writing expository prose. In preparing their own speeches, they get experience in analyzing poetry and organizing ideas. By using the tape recorder, the students overcome their fear of speaking to a group and obviate the embarrassment they normally feel about reading poetry aloud to their peers. Finally, having successfully given this lecture on tape gives many of them the confidence to speak well when later in the course they make a report or read aloud before the class. Thus the exercise of listening to and making a taped lecture helps students to develop their communication skills and their ability to analyze poetry. In short, their beloved boom boxes provide springboards to Pegasus.

Reference

Frost, Robert. 1949. The Figure a Poem Makes. In *Complete Poems of Robert Frost*. New York: Henry Holt.

5 A Talk Show with Class

Madeleine Myers
MacArthur High School
Irving, Texas

In lieu of a major test on *Great Expectations* in my ninth-grade English class, I have designed a group activity that calls for more than rote learning and passive reading and that involves creative thinking at all levels of communication: a talk show. This activity shows students that extending their thinking can be fun, and the assignment forces a closer reading of the text than a major test would require. To prepare for the activity, I divide the class into groups of six to eight and assign each group three or four "guests" (major characters in the novel) to be interviewed, three products or services taken from the novel to advertise (details of setting), and three "news items" (major events in the plot) to cover in their program. Each group is expected to develop these elements into a fifteen-minute talk show with commercials and a brief "newsbreak."

After choosing a project coordinator and a host for the talk show, the groups are instructed to develop an interview with each guest/ character that includes questions and answers covering significant events, personalities, motives, etc., in the novel. (Example: "Estella, why did you treat Pip so cruelly when you both were children?"). Commercials (e.g., for Joe's forge or Pumblechook's corn) and newsbreaks (e.g., "Convicted Felon Escapes," "Young Gentleman Foils Abduction Scheme") should reflect details discovered in close reading (e.g., the location of Clarriker's branch offices) and a knowledge of elements of fiction. The show must also be titled and be developed in the style of one of today's popular talk shows.

I set aside three or four class days to work on the project. Students are expected to develop visual aids: props, settings, title, product names and illustrations, credits, etc. Some reluctant readers are induced by peer pressure to complete the novel. Reading and re-reading, vision and revision result. Motivation develops in some borderline students when given the opportunity to make a nontraditional contribution: some nonreaders are excellent artists or actors, and enjoy involving their own special talent in the project. To further stimulate interest and develop listening skills, I encourage questions from the audience and assign those questions extra-credit points. An ambitious class might also videotape the production, if time and resources permit, and critique the project after viewing the videotape.

The evaluation of each project should involve the entire class. To promote active listening, I provide an evaluation form to each member of the audience, while the performing group completes another individualized self-evaluation. The latter is a confidential form that lists each group member by name and provides for ranking or grading each member's participation in the project. The self-evaluation includes an evaluation of the project as a whole and a statement of how the project might have been improved or changed. These evaluations are usually refreshingly candid, and are very useful in enabling the teacher to assign a fair grade. The teacher's final evaluation is a double one: a group grade and an individual grade based on preparation, faithfulness to the text, originality, overall smoothness and delivery, organization, and completeness (all assigned characters, products, and events must be covered). Superior acting, audiovisual techniques, and inclusion of more complex fictional elements (e.g., foreshadowing, irony, figurative language, and theme) earn bonus points.

Enthusiasm for the project runs high, and students usually claim to learn more about the book from this activity than they might have from studying for the usual objective test. The success of this assignment is reflected in their scores on the novel portion of the six-weeks' test, in which the objective format is used.

This assignment readily lends itself to other novels or epics and not only involves all levels of cognitive activity but also develops critical thinking, writing, and oral skills.

6 The Student-Centered Classroom: Speaking and Listening in American Literature

Barbara J. Osburg
Parkway North High School
Creve Coeur, Missouri

For years I agonized over and complained about the unwillingness of my students to participate in, or even to prepare for, my American Literature class. I teach high school juniors who are usually too apathetic to read their assignments, too laid-back or frightened to respond even if they have read them, and too pragmatically upwardly mobile to listen even if others might probe the deeper questions which literature invites—or so it seemed. But they have begun speaking and listening in my class in the last few years. Why? Because they are speaking and listening to one another, not to me.

Like most teachers, I give homework reading assignments from an anthology or a handout. I used to spend my class time "going over" these readings, which meant explaining what my students invariably called the "hidden meanings" behind the difficult prose they had muddled through (or failed to muddle through). Now, though, each reading assignment entails several student responsibilities in addition to perusal of the text, and these responsibilities take the form of responses. Students are required to write down and bring to class a quote that intrigued them, a question which puzzled them, or an insight they would like to share (these form the basis of the group-discussion component of class on the following day).

On many days, two student leaders run the two parts of class—journal sharing and group discussion. Different students are assigned the roles of journal-assigner/sharing-moderator and class discussion leader each day (these positions can be voluntary at first, but everyone must take a turn eventually). This process gets me out of the position of picking on people. It also forces students to see how difficult running a class discussion can be, and forces them to respond out of peer pressure as well as out of the need for a good participation grade. On some days, students actually conduct lessons themselves, seeing the classroom from the other side of the front desk. For my part, I get to see the classroom from the students' side, sitting in a student desk and noting participation points (if the discussion becomes too lively—as it often does—I might even forget to note the points).

Ground Rules

A few ground rules at the beginning of the semester set expectations for behavior and provide guidance to the student leaders and the rest of the class:

1. Calling on persons must be done fairly and equitably, not capriciously or vindictively. In other words, discussion leaders cannot protect their friends from involvement or unfairly give them too much attention; also they cannot call on people in order to embarrass them or to get even with them.
2. Everyone must listen when someone is reading aloud or speaking, and the speakers must speak loudly enough to be heard by everyone.
3. During journal sharing, before calling on the next respondent, discussion leaders must summarize each person's journal response as a check on listening and clarity of communication. During class discussion, students wishing to respond to another's comments must first briefly summarize those comments before stating their own positions. (For example, students might begin their comments with "I see. You think Beatrice meant to entrap Giovanni. I believe her when she says she 'thought only to love' him.")
4. The discussion leaders must act primarily as moderators and summarizers, not as the focus of discussion.

These ground rules help to set standards for good group conduct, and I can always bail the leaders out if they get into a tough situation. The rules also serve to remind me of my need to stay out of the way and let my students learn about literature.

The Journal Component

Typically, as the class periods begin, the designated journal-assigners write on the board a stimulating starter for the ten-minute journal period. Since I give points for length, I can check for that shortly before time is called and save myself from having to lug these monstrous journals home. At the end of the ten minutes, the journal-assigners become sharing-moderators, eliciting responses from students, who may read aloud from their journal entries or just talk about what they wrote while the sharing-moderators encourage others to respond. The moderators close the discussion when they feel most of the class have had their say. This procedure guarantees oral response because the members of the class have responses ready in the form of journal entries. Even the very taciturn can at least read their entries. And what about listening? Remember that one of the ground rules for the leaders is that they must briefly summarize the last person's response before calling on the next. And students wishing to respond to another's comments must first briefly summarize those comments before stating their own positions.

The Discussion Component

After the journal sharing is completed, or about halfway through the period (I help the moderators keep track of time), the discussion leaders conduct class discussion in a number of ways—small-group sharing of written responses, large-group sharing (which is like the journal format), focus on a few selected responses, reading aloud, recitation, acting out dramatic pieces, or any other stimulating approach to generating thought and discussion. Leaders choose the format for discussion but use the written homework responses as the matter for discussion. Once again, the ground rules are in effect: summarizing is required to ensure good listening and clear communication, I am no longer the focus of the discussion, and students take responsibility for the class. I am the keeper of the points. I sit and make note of who responds and make sure that those called on have done their homework. Participation counts in my class, and I am freed from center stage to attend to it.

Individual Presentations

The final unit of the year forces my students' speaking skills to a more formal level. They have learned to respond, they have learned to be articulate. Now they must also gather and convey information, hold the center stage for a few moments, and maintain poise in a performer-audience situation: each of them must prepare and teach one of the twentieth-century poems from our anthology. I use poetry for this assignment because I love it and students often say they hate it, and because a poem is short enough that I can make students responsible for an explanation of every word of the text. They sign up for poems on a first-come first-served basis and are scheduled for presentation dates which correspond to the chronology of the poems (our American Literature course is a traditional survey one semester long). Students must research the background of the author as well as his or her aesthetic; they must read, not recite by memory, the poem aloud with expression; and they must explain the poem, accounting for every word. They may bring in any visual aids necessary to clarify their presentation of the poet or the poem: a picture of Amy Lowell and of traditional seventeenth-century female dress for "Patterns," a shell and other items for e. e. cummings' "maggie and milly and molly and may," pictures of the moon walk for Robert Hayden's "Astronauts." The presentations may be as elaborate or as simple as the students choose. They may use the entire period or any part of it (if I am short of time, I limit the presentations to fifteen minutes and schedule them accordingly). But on their scheduled day, the students teach the class.

When a student has finished his or her presentation, each of the other students in the class must write a brief critique, and five students selected at random ahead of time must ask questions. I also grade the presentation on content and performance, but the presenters are often more eager (and anxious) about the critiques of their peers than about my evaluations. Some make overheads and show videotapes to help clarify the poems for their classmates; some simply share the poet's bio, read the poem aloud, and do a textual analysis. Some stumble and blush; others rise to the occasion like full professors of their subjects. I am not the expert on Hayden or Mari Evans or Adrienne Rich or Amiri Baraka; they are the experts, and I watch each semester in amazement and delight. Of all of the American literature we study, the piece each student remembers best, knows best, and loves most is the poem he or she teaches to the class.

Conclusion

Many students are frightened at the beginning of my class about having to speak in front of others, about having to monitor class discussion, and about having to teach a poem. But by the end of the class, they are more confident, louder, clearer, and more articulate.

They even begin reading their assignments because their peers will be calling on them and responding to and evaluating their ideas about the literature—because someone other than a teacher will be listening to them talk about what they think. Admittedly, I sometimes must sacrifice my favorite interpretation of a given piece because it does not emerge from the leader's discussion and I cannot dominate the class period with my own concerns. I leave a few pieces to myself ("The Hollow Men," "Out of the Cradle Endlessly Rocking," "The Birthmark," and "The Open Boat") because I need to teach, too, and because I love to teach those pieces. But the best experience of teaching is to see students grow into independence because of what we have taught them. And I can sometimes best teach them that independence by giving them the responsibility of teaching.

7 Analyzing Literature through Collaborative Speaking

Göran "George" Moberg
Borough of Manhattan Community College
City University of New York

When I began this peer-group experiment about three years ago, my chief aim was to help my community college students improve their writing in an introduction-to-literature course. Now that the method, which I'm going to describe in some detail here, is fairly well-oiled, the writing component is still important. However, I think we see the greatest benefits in the students' increased confidence in *speaking* about literature and *listening* to other students' speaking about literature.

Here is the process, step by step:

Groups

During the first week of classes, the students are divided into four or five groups of five or six each. These groups are permanent for the term; only occasionally do I make judicious changes in the group formations. A few years ago I used to wait a week until I got to know the students a little and then formed groups according to my notion of an academically sound mix. I've now stopped playing God. I seem to be getting at least as good groupings by allowing the students to select their own peers.

Reading Assignments

Instead of always assigning the same material to the whole class, I usually assign different poems or stories to each group. For instance, the groups might receive one sonnet by Wordsworth, one by Byron, one by Shelley, and one by Keats, respectively. Or they might be assigned to read different sonnets by Shakespeare. The same would go for short stories. Toward the end of the term, when the groups are working smoothly together, we do drama, with each group taking on one of the following: *Antigone, Macbeth, A Doll's House, Pygmalion,* and *Death of a Salesman.* This stage in the process is the most exciting because we are treated to actual performances of key scenes in the plays. These shows have ranged from simple readings by seated students to elaborate productions up front with costumes, lighting, and special sound effects. I require nothing, only suggest. Peer pressure is productive.

One caution: I do not use texts that have an elaborate academic apparatus; since my course constitutes one extended exercise in generating one's own judgments, the barer the presentation of primary text material, the better. The class procedures themselves will present variety and challenge, and I'm always there to supply background and guidance.

Journals

The students also have to keep a careful record of their readings in special notebooks referred to as journals. The system, which I call "double-entry journal-keeping," goes like this: on the left-hand page of the journal, the students write an objective summary description of their reading. Then on the facing right side of their journal-notebook they write down their personal reactions to their reading. I encourage crisp, neutral writing on the left side; on the right side, expansive free-writing with emotional risk-taking.

Group Discussion

Early in the semester, I begin each class with a brief lecture—either an overview of what the class is doing or an explanation of some technical literary point. I also offer suggestions for a focus in the group discussions coming up. As the weeks go by, however, my own talking gradually yields to the primary activities of the course.

For about a quarter of an hour (depending on the length of the period), the members of each group—acting like a workshop—discuss the day's reading assignment among each other. The starting point most of the time is the journal entry that one of the students reads aloud to the rest (they take turns). Then the others respond either impromptu or by reading from their own journals. Part of the clearly defined task is to organize their group presentation.

Group Presentations

The group presentations are the highlights of the collaborative speaking method. Each group in turn presents its story or poem to the whole class. The group members speak on a rotating basis. First, one member of a group begins with an objective summary or description of the assigned reading. (It's important that exact page references to the text are given so the rest of the class can follow in their books and mark them up, as will be explained shortly.) Next, someone else in the same group offers a personal response. When a group has not reached interpretative consensus (which happens often), several members will read from their journals or make arguments in favor of their views. At this point students in other groups are invited to ask questions. Although, as the instructor, I chair these sessions and sometimes interject clarifying information, I basically try to stay out of the proceedings. Initiative, self-reliance, and courage are what I ask for—and get.

While one group is giving its report to the class, the other students are following the presentations both by listening and by following in their texts. They are encouraged to underline, to make entries in their own journals, and to ask questions—which often results in heated debates that are far more spontaneous than arranged "panel discussions." (I've been humbled to note that many students listen to their peers' literary analyses more eagerly than to mine.) One result of the process is that the students become familiar with material that they have not actually been assigned to study as homework.

Tests

My students write their essay exams with open books and open journals. In fact, in support of their literary discussion, they are *required* to quote from their own journals, as well as from the primary sources in their texts. Though they're responsible only for the texts assigned to their own group, they're encouraged (bonus points offered!) to include in their written discussion remarks about material presented by other groups. In fact, I've noted that the most successful students actually go home and read literary pieces they heard about in class but were not required to read in their own group.

Discipline

I tell the class at the beginning of the course that in the final essay they will be asked to describe and evaluate the work presented in their group by each of their named peers; knowing this, few students try to get a free ride since they apparently believe their classmates' evaluation to be more rigorous than mine.

Further, because the students actually *need* honest and full journals to function in the group, in the class, and on the essay exams, it's not necessary for me frequently to look over their shoulders into their journals. I do not directly grade the journals, though some teachers might choose to do so. (When specific students occasionally plead with me to read sections of their journals, however, I readily comply.) I find quizzes unnecessary. The course grade depends on performance in group/class and on the half-a-dozen essay exams that they write.

Conclusion

Improved writing was my original aim, and indeed, the journal-writing seems to have helped improve my students' essay-writing. But the emerging by-products—which I think have become primary benefits—are (1) better speaking and listening in class as a result of the journal-writing, and (2) better analytical essay-writing as a result of all the intense speaking in the workshop-like groups. Above all, students gain confidence in their ability to read literature and express opinions; as a result, I seldom get my own opinions lamely given back to me. Instead I hear genuine student voices. I see writing styles that struggle to be born.

8 Talking about Books*

Margaret Hutchingson
Pierremont School
Manchester, Missouri

In an effort to focus on independent reading, oral language, and critical thinking skills, the Parkway School District, in 1980, implemented a program entitled TALKING ABOUT BOOKS. The program provides class sets of paperback books to teachers. Some 175 titles from current children's literature, selected by Parkway teachers and librarians, are used with heterogeneously grouped classes in kindergarten through tenth grade.

TALKING ABOUT BOOKS extends the work already being done in reading and writing to the areas of listening and speaking. For most people, effective group- discussion skills are essential tools throughout their lives, since groups are the basic operational units of our society. These skills, however, do not come automatically. They must be learned and practiced regularly.

The aim of the TALKING ABOUT BOOKS program is to guide children to help one another to learn through reading books and then discussing basic questions in them. The books used are not to be "taught"; rather, they are to be read independently, generally outside of class time. For this program, the emphasis is on thoughtful responses to ideas in the book brought out in peer-group discussions, not on literal comprehension or retention of factual information. Most boys and girls have expressed the feeling that they understand and enjoy books more after sharing ideas. Poor or reluctant readers have added that it was the first time they gained true pleasure from reading.

Following students' reading of a book chosen by the teacher as appropriate to the class's needs, the children are divided into two groups for the purpose of discussing responses to open-ended infer-

---

* This chapter first appeared in slightly different form in *The Pennsylvania Speech Communication Annual* © 1987, Vol. XLIII. It is reprinted with permission.

ential questions. One group is led by the teacher; the other, by the librarian or other trained adult leader. These group discussions are videotaped. Teachers play back selected portions of the videotapes to the participants so that they can observe and evaluate their own behaviors in light of predetermined criteria.* These criteria are defined on student self-evaluation forms suitable for the particular age level (reproduced at the end of this chapter). The only "testing" in the program occurs in the discussion itself, after which each child is asked to evaluate his or her performance in speaking, listening, and generating ideas.

In the course of the discussion, a few of the main themes are examined thoroughly. Boys and girls are given the opportunity to express their opinions about questions posed by the leader and to listen to what other students have to say. The leader does not react in any way to suggest that a student's response was "right" or "wrong." The children may ask questions, too, but only the other boys and girls may offer answers. The leader also encourages participants to agree or disagree with the author or with fellow discussants, and to support their opinions with reasons based on their reading. The students are encouraged to make their statements and direct their questions to one another rather than to the adult leader.

An important element in a book discussion is wait time, a period of silence after a question has been asked to give participants time to reflect on their responses. A second wait time occurs after a question has been answered. Teachers using wait time in their classes have found that it results in increases in both the number of students responding and the length of their responses, and that many students will add to or amplify their answers during these brief periods of silence.

The self-evaluations that are completed by each participating student following a discussion are designed to increase attention to speaking and listening skills, as well as to thoughts and ideas. On an increasingly difficult scale as students advance through the grades, emphasis is placed on a refinement of elements of the speech process: vocal clarity, articulation, fluency, appropriate volume, rate, speech etiquette, and confidence. Listening skills focus on the development of an active listening attitude by emphasizing attention, interpretative listening to teacher questions and peer responses, listening for ideas

---

* David Fletcher ("Oral Language and the Language Arts Teacher," *Language Arts* 58, no. 2 [February 1981]: 219–24) summarizes the work of Emma Plattor and others who have pointed out that tests of oral language "should specify the objectives for listening and speaking in terms of knowledge, skills, and attitudes; audience, situation, and purpose; cognition and affect; and casual, informal, and formal language use."

as well as facts, weighing information, focusing on the speaker, ignoring distractions, asking questions, and giving feedback.

Three Fifth Graders

Among one fifth-grade group who used the program, the three students who made the highest gains in total reading are interesting examples. Beyond the measurable gains in reading, the self-evaluations submitted by these three fifth graders show three kinds of gains that are less easy to measure but which reflect objectives of equal importance to reading in the elementary language arts classroom. Gary, Charla, and Paul are students of varying abilities who gained proficiency in critical thinking, social consciousness, and reading for pleasure.

Improved Critical Thinking Skills

Gary was an above-average student in every subject area. His social skills were highly developed; he was respected as a leader by his peers. In the course of the book discussions, Gary came to recognize that thinking about the answers to higher-level questions stretched his mind and challenged his imagination.

After the first discussion, Gary wrote that the thing he liked most was "answering the questions." By the fourth discussion he "found it difficult to listen to people who didn't explain their ideas," and noted that he needed to "think harder." Gary wrote, "This discussion helped me to talk and understand more."

"Listening to others' ideas" was noted as the highlight of the seventh discussion by Gary. He set as a goal for the next discussion "to think and talk harder." Subsequently he felt that "it took too long for me to express my ideas," and that it was necessary to "listen harder." These statements show Gary's recognition of the total group's increased facility in generating responses to open-ended questions. On his twelfth self-evaluation, Gary wrote, "The discussion helped me to see attitudes toward others."

Increased Social Awareness

Charla, a fifth grader of average ability, was eager, willing, and highly motivated to learn. Following the first discussion, Charla noted on her self-evaluation that she spoke less than she should have, adding that the discussion helped her to see that she need not be "afraid to talk." Charla set fuller participation as her goal for the second discussion. In evaluating her performance, Charla felt that she contributed more than she should have "because I didn't bring other people that hadn't talked into the discussion."

As her goal for the third discussion, Charla set the encouragement of others, but she did not succeed and wrote, "I should bring other people into the discussion." By the fourth discussion, however, Charla commented that she did encourage others, although it was most difficult for her "to stop talking." It is interesting to note that Charla found that the thing she liked best about the discussion "was the part when we did a lot of piggy-backing" (i.e., building upon other students' ideas). Active interchange of ideas involving many discussants was exciting to her.

Following the fifth discussion, Charla again commented, "I just didn't let other people [contribute] who didn't talk enough." Setting as her goal to decrease the number of her own responses in the sixth discussion, Charla checked that she contributed less than she should have (see the Intermediate Grades self-evaluation form). "The thing I liked best about this discussion," she wrote, was "that people who don't talk a lot came into the discussion." Charla saw a cause-and-effect relationship between her talking less and the functioning of the entire group. In subsequent discussions, Charla found a comfortable level where she could feel she "talked enough but not too much." She continued to be very aware of her classmates, specifying at one point that "Kim and Kristine came into the discussion."

Developed Love for Reading

When Paul entered the fifth grade he was in the lowest reading group. He did consistently poor work on the reading comprehension sections of several standardized tests. The basal reader in which Paul worked was a full year below that of average fifth graders in the group. Paul lacked motivation and by his own admission did not enjoy recreational reading. His responses to questions about the stories in the reading text were shallow and did not give evidence of thoughtful reading. Paul had rarely read an entire book appropriate to his age level; the library books he chose were either "easy readers" or those that included many illustrations and a minimum of text.

Paul contributed very little to the first two book discussions. He indicated on his self-evaluation that although he had read the books, he spoke less than he should have, adding, "I only talked when she [the leader] said my name." He also wrote that he did not like to talk out loud and that the thing he liked most about the discussions was "watching our self on TV."

By the third discussion, Paul wrote that he had enjoyed the book read by the group and noted that the discussion helped him to see "how my ideas are different" from his classmates. Paul began participating comfortably during the fourth discussion. He wrote that the discussion helped him to see that he could talk out loud. By the fifth discussion, he circled, for the first time, that he had contributed his fair share. He wrote that he had set a goal to participate more actively and "stayed with it." "This discussion helped me to see," Paul continued, "that I can talk out loud." He even became aware of his fellow participants, noting that it was difficult for him to encourage those who had not spoken, "but I did it anyway."

In filling out his self-evaluation for the sixth discussion, Paul again noted that he had enjoyed the book. There was evidence of Paul's newfound enjoyment of recreational reading at home as well as in the classroom. He chose to read during independent work times and checked out a variety of books from the library. By the seventh discussion, Paul wrote that "books are fun to read," and by the eighth discussion he was participating so much in the discussions that he wrote, "The hardest thing for me to do in the discussion was keeping still."

By the end of the fifth-grade year, Paul, out of a class of twenty-five students, had submitted the second largest number of book reports—fifty-four. His SRA scores for Total Reading in the fall of the sixth-grade year indicated a gain of seventy-four points. Most notable, however, was Paul's changed attitude toward reading, which can be attributed both to the types of books used in the TALKING ABOUT BOOKS program and to his recognition of underlying meanings brought out by the type of inferential questions asked.

Conclusion

The TALKING ABOUT BOOKS program is now in its ninth year in the Parkway School District, where it has won wide acceptance by both teachers and parents. The books are perceived as a valuable adjunct to the reading and language curricula. Teachers have also found correlations with topics in social studies, science, and even mathematics. The oral language strand of the program presents a discussion technique that teachers employ in other group-involvement situations. Many students have enhanced their critical thinking skills as well. And, as in the case studies of Gary, Charla, and Paul, spin-offs into other areas vital to children's growth and maturity as both students and people continue to be noticed.

NAME_____

SCHOOL_____

DATE_____

DISCUSSION TOPIC_____

FORM #1-P

Primary Grades

STUDENT SELF EVALUATION

I WAS A GOOD SPEAKER

1. I spoke so everyone could hear me.	YES	NO
2. I looked at people when I spoke to them.	YES	NO
3. I contributed my fair share to the discussion.	YES	NO

____more than I should have   Why?_____

_____

____less than I should have   Why?_____

_____

4. I feel people in the group paid attention to what I said.	YES	NO
5. I was afraid to talk during the discussion.	YES	NO

I WAS A GOOD LISTENER

6. I listened to each student.	YES	NO
7. I looked at each speaker.	YES	NO
8. I interrupted other speakers.	YES	NO
9. I thought about what others said.	YES	NO

I SHARED MY IDEAS WELL

10. I had read the book.	YES	NO
11. I explained my ideas clearly.	YES	NO
12. I backed up my ideas with reasons.	YES	NO
13. I helped keep the discussion on the topic.	YES	NO

NAME_____

SCHOOL_____

DATE_____

DISCUSSION TOPIC_____

FORM #1-1

Intermediate Grades 4–6

STUDENT SELF EVALUATION

SPEAKING SKILLS

1. I spoke as clearly as I could.	YES	NO
2. I think that everyone in the group could hear me.	YES	NO
3. I looked at people when I spoke to them.	YES	NO
4. If I did not understand, I would have been willing to ask questions.	YES	NO
5. I contributed my fair share to the discussion.	YES	NO

___more than I should have*

___less than I should have*

* You may give a reason for your answer in the space below.

6. I feel people in the group paid attention to what I said.	YES	NO
7. I was afraid to talk during the discussion.	YES	NO
8. I encouraged others.	YES	NO

LISTENING SKILLS

9. I thought it was important to listen to each student.	YES	NO
10. I looked at each speaker.	YES	NO
11. I listened politely by not interrupting.	YES	NO
12. I was willing to listen to others' opinions.	YES	NO
13. I was easily distracted.	YES	NO
14. I accepted others' ideas without thinking about them.	YES	NO
15. I could understand other students' ideas.	YES	NO

(*continued on following page*)

IDEAS

16.	I was prepared for the discussion.	YES	NO
17.	I think that everyone could understand my ideas.	YES	NO
18.	I backed up my ideas with reasons.	YES	NO
19.	I built on other students' ideas ("piggy-backed").	YES	NO
20.	When I disagreed, I backed up my reasons with information from the book.	YES	NO
21.	I helped keep the discussion on the topic.	YES	NO

NAME＿＿＿＿＿＿＿＿＿＿＿＿＿

SCHOOL＿＿＿＿＿＿＿＿＿＿＿＿

DATE＿＿＿＿＿＿＿＿＿＿＿＿＿

DISCUSSION TOPIC＿＿＿＿＿＿

FORM #1-1S

Junior High School

STUDENT SELF EVALUATION

SPEAKING SKILLS

1. I spoke as clearly as I could.   YES   NO

2. I think that everyone in the group could hear me.   YES   NO

3. I looked at people when I spoke to them.   YES   NO

4. I contributed my fair share to the discussion.   YES   NO

＿more than I should have   Why?＿＿＿＿＿＿＿＿＿＿＿＿＿

＿less than I should have   Why?＿＿＿＿＿＿＿＿＿＿＿＿＿

5. If I did not understand, I would have been willing
   to admit it.   YES   NO

6. I was willing to ask questions.   YES   NO

7. If I disagreed, I felt free to do so.   YES   NO

8. I feel people in the group paid attention to what
   I said.   YES   NO

9. I was afraid to talk during the discussion.   YES   NO

10. I was considerate of others.   YES   NO

11. I encouraged others.   YES   NO

LISTENING SKILLS

12. I thought it was important to listen to each
    student.   YES   NO

13. I looked at each speaker.   YES   NO

14. I allowed others to finish.   YES   NO

15. I allowed others to speak.   YES   NO

16. I listened actively (didn't fake attention or day-
    dream).   YES   NO

17. I was willing to listen to others' opinions.   YES   NO

18. I distinguished between information from the
    book and people's own opinions.   YES   NO

(*continued on following page*)

IDEAS

19. I was prepared for the discussion.	YES	NO
20. I think that everyone could understand my ideas.	YES	NO
21. I supported my ideas with direct citation and/or incidents from the book.	YES	NO
22. I backed up my ideas with reasons.	YES	NO
23. I built on other students' ideas ("piggy-backed").	YES	NO
24. I examined ideas before accepting or rejecting them.	YES	NO
25. When I disagreed, I backed up my reasons with information from the book.	YES	NO
26. I helped keep the discussion on the topic.	YES	NO

NAME_____

SCHOOL_____

DATE_____

DISCUSSION TOPIC_____

FORM #1-HS

High School

STUDENT SELF EVALUATION

SPEAKING SKILLS

1. I spoke clearly and articulately.	YES	NO
2. My voice volume was appropriate.	YES	NO
3. I maintained eye contact with my audience.	YES	NO
4. I was an active contributor.	YES	NO
5. I was willing to admit if I did not understand.	YES	NO
6. I initiated questions and/or explanations.	YES	NO
7. I felt free to disagree.	YES	NO
8. Others listened to my contributions.	YES	NO
9. I felt free to talk during the discussion.	YES	NO
10. I was considerate of others.	YES	NO
11. I encouraged and supported other group members.	YES	NO
12. I encouraged others to participate.	YES	NO
13. I controlled unnecessary vocalizations.	YES	NO

LISTENING SKILLS

14. I thought it was important to listen to everyone.	YES	NO
15. I maintained eye contact with each speaker.	YES	NO
16. I refrained from interrupting others.	YES	NO
17. I refrained from dominating the discussion.	YES	NO
18. I actively listened to all contributions.	YES	NO
19. I maintained an open mind toward others' opinions.	YES	NO
20. I distinguished between fact and opinion.	YES	NO
21. I focused my attention on the discussion at all times.	YES	NO

(*continued on following page*)

THINKING SKILLS

22.	I was prepared for the discussion.	YES	NO
23.	I presented my ideas clearly.	YES	NO
24.	I supported my ideas with direct citations and/or incidents from the book.	YES	NO
25.	I supported my ideas logically.	YES	NO
26.	I extended on others' ideas.	YES	NO
27.	I examined ideas before accepting or rejecting them.	YES	NO
28.	When I disagreed, I supported my thoughts with references from the book.	YES	NO
29.	My ideas were relevant to the topic.	YES	NO
30.	My ideas demonstrated insight.	YES	NO

9 Personification in Children's Literature: Identifying, Analyzing, and Performing

Donna E. Norton
Texas A&M University

Stimulating the imagination, bringing delight by seeing likenesses among unlike objects, making the abstract concrete, and expressing larger ideas in briefer terms are a few of the reasons for encouraging children to appreciate, to use, and to interact with figurative language. Authors of literature and poetry for children, especially authors of award-winning books, rely heavily on figurative language to enhance the impact and the beauty of the text. Unfortunately, figurative language implies other than literal meanings; it is therefore difficult for many children to understand.

Personification, a form of figurative language in which animals, objects, or concepts are given human characteristics, is found in literature ranging from picture storybooks for the youngest children to poetry and novels for adult audiences. Personification provides an excellent introduction to figurative language and lends itself to analysis and performance.

The following activities show that children from second through eighth grade can understand and appreciate personification in literature. These activities ask students to (1) identify personification during listening and observation, (2) discuss and analyze personification following listening and observation, and (3) perform tasks that enhance understanding of and appreciation for personification. Before beginning any of the activities, the teacher should clarify the meaning of personification through examples.

The Little House (Personification of Objects)

The illustrations and the text of Virginia Lee Burton's *The Little House* (1942) show how an author and an illustrator can effectively use personification. Prior to oral reading, ask students to listen and look for answers to the following questions:

1. What pronoun is used when the author talks about the house? Could the word be used when talking about a person?
2. What actions can the house do that are similar to your actions?
3. What feelings does the house express that are similar to your feelings?
4. What causes the house to have each of these feelings?
5. When have you had similar feelings?
6. How do the illustrations help you understand the house's feelings and character?

Following the oral reading, students discuss the above questions. When doing the activity with younger children teachers can read the whole text for appreciation and continuity and then reread and discuss individual pages. With older students teachers can stress that illustrating and writing picture storybooks for children are adult occupations. In addition to searching for evidence of personification, older students can look for reasons why Burton's book won the Caldecott Medal for illustrations.

This discussion phase emphasizes that the house is always called "she"; that personified actions include watching, waiting, thinking, hearing, feeling, and dreaming; that personified emotions include happiness, curiosity, surprise, sadness, loneliness, and fright; that the bright, cheery country made the house happy, while the dirty, crowded city caused opposite feelings; that children frequently experience similar feelings; and that the illustrations show the house with corresponding expressions and rely on colors to enhance the mood.

During the performance phase, younger students pantomime the feelings expressed by the house and create conversations that might occur between the house and her city or country neighbors. Interesting conversational partners for the house include the horseless carriages, the subway, and the moving truck. This activity extends an understanding of personification as children consider how these objects might respond if they had the house's personified qualities.

Older students also benefit by creating conversations or by telling the story from the point of view of one of the objects. Now they must consider how they could effectively personify a subway, a carriage, an apartment, or a truck. What comparisons would they make? Poems such as Charles Malam's "Steam Shovel" and William Jay Smith's "The Toaster," found in the poetry anthology *Reflections on a Gift of Watermelon Pickle* (1967), enhance the discussion and show students how poets effectively personify objects.

Picnic (Personification of Animals)

Emily Arnold McCully's *Picnic* (1984) is an excellent source for developing relationships between personification and illustrations. The wordless text forces children to observe the detailed illustrations and to produce their own text that includes the personified mice responding to setting, conflict, plot development, characterization, and point of view. This resulting literary style is obviously rich with personification.

During the observational phase children look carefully at each of the illustrations. They consider the following questions:

1. How does the illustrator let you know immediately that mice will have at least some personified characteristics?

2. What actions are similar to your actions? How does the illustrator show these actions? How would you describe these actions in personified terms?

3. What feelings or emotions do these mice seem to be expressing? How does the illustrator show these feelings? How would you describe these feelings in personified terms?

The discussion following the observation emphasizes that the illustrator includes drawings of mice living in a house, riding in a truck, and preparing to play baseball; that the artist shows mice driving a truck, preparing the picnic setting, playing ball, strumming an instrument, hugging each other, and crying; that the artist depicts happiness through mice jumping for joy, loneliness and maybe fear through tears, determination and self-reliance through hunting for food, worry through searching for a missing son, and love through the mice's responses when finding the lost child.

With this book the performance phase includes many rich possibilities. In addition to creating a story to accompany the illustrations, students have created dialogues among the mice as they prepare for the picnic, as they play games at the picnic site, as they search for the missing mouse, and as they experience a happy reunion. Students have developed understanding of personified emotions as they create the inner thoughts of the mouse who is lost or the thoughts of Mother Mouse and other family members when they discover that a family member is missing.

Older students may expand their understanding of when personification is appropriate and when it is less desirable by comparing fantasy in which animals are appropriately personified with contemporary realistic fiction and informational books in which animals should not be personified. For this comparison develop a chart that includes the following information:*

	Personified Fantasy	Realistic Fiction Nonfiction
Characters:	Animals behave like people, with human thoughts, motives, and emotions.	Animals behave like animals. Information agrees with animal behavior.
Setting:	Can be imaginary.	World as we know it.
Plot and Content:	Animal conflicts similar to human conflicts.	Observable animal behaviors. Life cycle of animal.
Illustrations:	Animals may be dressed like people and show emotions.	Photographs and drawings of actual animals in real surroundings.

Begin the discussion and analysis with comparisons between *Picnic* and an informational book about mice such as Oxford Scientific Films' *Harvest Mouse* (1982). Analyze and compare the characters, setting, story content, and illustrations. Consider why each is effective for its own purpose. Additional animal comparisons for this activity include Anthony Browne's personified *Gorilla* (1983) and Carol Fenner's nonfictional *Gorilla, Gorilla* (1973); Beatrix Potter's personified *The Tale of Peter Rabbit* (1902, 1986) or Robert Lawson's *Rabbit Hill* (1944) and Lilo Hess's nonfictional *Diary of a Rabbit* (1982); and E. B. White's personified *Charlotte's Web* (1952) and Jack Denton Scott's nonfictional *The Book of the Pig* (1981). Personified fantasy and realistic fictional comparisons include Dr. Seuss's personified *The Cat in the Hat* (1957) and Sheila Burnford's realistic fiction *The Incredible Journey* (1961) and George Selden's personified *Harry Cat's Pet Puppy* (1975) and Jim Kjelgaard's realistic fiction *Big Red* (1945, 1956).

Hiawatha (Personification of Nature)

Henry Wadsworth Longfellow's *Hiawatha* is available in numerous sources as well as in two shorter versions illustrated by Errol Le Cain

---

* For a more extensive discussion of differences between fantasy and realistic fiction, see Norton's *Through the Eyes of a Child: An Introduction to Children's Literature,* 1987, pp. 379, 408–9.

(1984) and Susan Jeffers (1983). When this activity is done with older students who have backgrounds in other types of poetic elements, the discussion and performance can include rhythm, imagery, and alliteration as well as personification. The activity as described emphasizes how these literary elements and illustrations enhance the appreciation of poetry with older students.

Before sharing one of the illustrated versions of the poem with students, draw the beginning of a literary web on the board. With "HIAWATHA" in the center, draw spokes going to Personification, Imagery, Alliteration, and Rhythm. (This poem may require several readings, with the first reading merely for pleasure and general feelings.) Ask the students to listen and to look for answers to the following questions:

1. How is the setting (nature) personified? What words does the poet use to personify nature?

2. What image does the personification create in your mind?

3. What images are created by descriptive terms?

4. What examples of alliteration do you hear? How do these words enhance the poem?

5. Listen to the rhythm of the poem. What words help reinforce the rhythm? What impression does the rhythm create? Why is it effective for the poem?

6. How do the illustrations match or enhance the personification and the imagery of the text?

During the discussion and analysis phase fill in the information on the web and discuss the images created or enhanced by each literary element. Share with the students the fact that Le Cain's *Hiawatha's Childhood* won the 1985 Kate Greenaway Medal for illustration in Great Britain. Ask them to consider whether Le Cain's sense of imagery might have influenced that choice. The web on page 48 was completed with eighth-grade students.

Choral arrangements of *Hiawatha* are excellent methods for highlighting personification and author's style. For example, readers theatre arrangements emphasize personification and characterization by providing narrator parts and various character roles. Character roles include lines for Nokomis, Hiawatha, pine trees, water, fireflies, owl and owlet, and Hiawatha's animal brothers. Both readers theatre and choral speaking arrangements enhance students' appreciation of the rhythmic quality of Longfellow's poem. We frequently accompany oral readings with a drum beat.

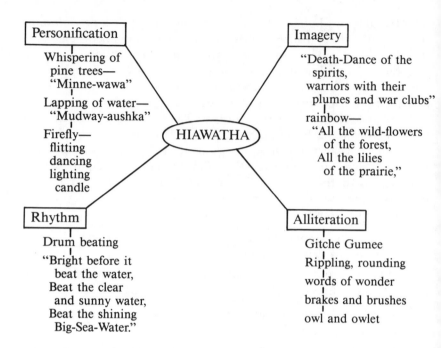

Choral arrangements also provide ways to analyze the effectiveness of poem divisions. Although the words are the same for both of the illustrated texts, Le Cain and Jeffers chose different divisions of the text. Consequently, different lines are grouped together. For example, the Le Cain version places the lines about fiery tresses and the spirits' death-dance on one page with an illustration in hot reds and oranges; the next page shows the frosty nights of winter and crowds of ghosts in icy whites and dark greens. In contrast, the Jeffers version places all of these lines on one page accompanied by shadowy ghostly figures. A page-a-group choral arrangement enhances the analysis of the two texts. For Le Cain's version the class is divided into fourteen groups; for Jeffers' version, ten groups. The students practice their assigned pages, present the total book as a choral arrangement, and consider the effectiveness of each division. Groups may try different divisions if they decide that neither text is the more effective.

During these activities students discover that personification enhances literature and their appreciation of the literature. They also discover that poetry is enjoyable.

References

Browne, Anthony. 1983. *Gorilla.* New York: Watts.

Burnfield, Sheila. 1961. *The Incredible Journey.* Boston: Little, Brown.

Burton, Virginia Lee. 1942. *The Little House.* Boston: Houghton Mifflin.

Dunning, Stephen, Edward Lueders, and Hugh Smith, eds. 1967. *Reflections on a Gift of Watermelon Pickle & Other Modern Verse.* New York: Lothrop, Lee & Shepard.

Fenner, Carol. 1973. *Gorilla, Gorilla.* New York: Random House.

Hess, Lilo. 1982. *Diary of a Rabbit.* New York: Scribner.

Kjelgaard, Jim. 1945, 1956. *Big Red.* New York: Holiday.

Lawson, Robert. 1944. *Rabbit Hill.* New York: Viking.

Longfellow, Henry Wadsworth. 1983. *Hiawatha.* Illustrated by Susan Jeffers. New York: Dial.

———. 1984. *Hiawatha's Children.* Illustrated by Errol Le Cain. New York: Farrar Straus & Giroux.

McCully, Emily Arnold. 1984. *Picnic.* New York: Harper and Row.

Norton, Donna E. 1987. *Through the Eyes of a Child: An Introduction to Children's Literature.* Columbus, Ohio: Merrill.

Oxford Scientific Films. 1982. *Harvest Mouse.* New York: Putnam.

Potter, Beatrix. 1902, 1986. *The Tale of Peter Rabbit.* New York: Warne.

Scott, Jack Denton. 1981. *The Book of the Pig.* New York: Putnam.

Selden, George. 1975. *Harry Cat's Pet Puppy.* New York: Farrar Straus & Giroux.

Seuss, Dr. 1957. *The Cat in the Hat.* New York: Random House.

White, E. B. 1952. *Charlotte's Web.* New York: Harper.

10 Who's Talking?

Dion Kempthorne
University of Wisconsin Center–Washington County

One important task in teaching prose fiction and creative writing is to help students understand that novels and short stories are not autobiographical reports. Students too often assume that the narrator or main character must be the author, and in their own writing frequently are constrained by their memory of what actually happened, thinking their stories must stick to the "facts" of personal experience. Although students should be taught the value of personal experience in reading and writing fiction, they need also to understand how point of view can make them better readers and writers.

The following activity asks students to demonstrate their comprehension of point of view by writing and then reading aloud a brief part of a story from an assigned viewpoint, and by listening to identify the viewpoints of pieces written and read by their classmates. This pattern of writing, reading aloud, and purposefully listening to their own stories helps them develop their creative and analytical skills and provides an excellent atmosphere for discussion. Since good writers and readers, like effective speakers and listeners, share concerns for focus and voice and vantage point, this exercise works well in literature and creative writing classes to show how the skills of the writer and reader (or speaker and listener) are interrelated. Demanding but enjoyable, this activity requires and encourages all the students to take an active part in a sound literary discussion; indeed, in short order most perform well as writers and readers, speakers and listeners, and individually and collectively as artists and critics.

Before starting this activity, the instructor should define several basic narrative viewpoints, such as omniscient, third-person limited, first person, and interior monologue, and illustrate each with passages from literary works. Textbooks often define and illustrate various viewpoints, but examples are of course easy to find elsewhere. For instance, part of the Molly Bloom section of *Ulysses* might be used to illustrate interior monologue, the opening of *Huckleberry Finn* to explain first person, and so on. Such samples should be made available to the class and read aloud to enable the students to see and hear the writing as it functions at once as literary text and speech. The instructor should also note some of the distinctions in style and effect of each viewpoint. This discussion of professional models helps the class see ways to write, read, and discuss their own work.

After the idea of viewpoint seems clear, the instructor should distribute a scene containing several characters and some central action. The scene can be as simple as the following: a man, about forty-five, in a business suit, is sitting with a woman, about twenty, at a table in a restaurant. Seated alone at a nearby table is a boy, about ten. Suddenly the woman stands and pours her drink over the man's head.

Such a scene should be enough to get the students started. Some will ask for more information, but most will be happy to provide further detail to make their stories unique. Later, they will see the extent to which the precision of detail depends on viewpoint and imagination.

Next the instructor should pass a box with slips of paper designating, say, the following viewpoints: omniscient, third-person man, third woman, third boy, first-person man, first woman, first boy, interior-monologue man, interior woman, interior boy. These ten angles may be repeated to suit larger classes, or in smaller classes students can be asked to write from more than one viewpoint; either way, significant variations in style and content will become an important part of the subsequent discussion. After drawing an individual assignment from the box, each student should write several lines (one hundred words or so) of a story in the randomly drawn viewpoint. When they have finished writing (10–15 minutes), they should take turns reading their passages aloud while the rest listen to identify the viewpoint.

This activity is most instructive because students learn by doing. They demonstrate their knowledge of viewpoint as writers who can speak in fictive voices, and demonstrate their understanding as readers who can listen with an educated ear. Drawing lots adds a sense of fun, fairness, and challenge because the students have to write in viewpoints different from their own. Reading aloud (speaking their pieces) lets them warm up their voices and indulge in some play-acting that creates a relaxed atmosphere for the open discussion of creative and critical notions. Sharing their writing quickly provides many examples of different viewpoints, and having to identify each viewpoint tests their listening skills. Moreover, the discussion of each piece provides each writer an immediate critique and requires all to explain their intentions and interpretations in precise terms of viewpoint.

Overall, the community effort (in a "name-that-tune" spirit) leads to a delightful process of discovery and understanding. Writing, reading, hearing, and discussing these little stories that are generated so quickly helps the students see ways to get started as artists and critics. Surprised and entertained by the different stories from one simple scene, they not only learn how much a story depends on viewpoint but also inevitably detect complications in viewpoint that lead to more sophisticated discussions of style and meaning. Most important, they learn that the work of the writer and that of the reader are ineluctably connected and ongoing, that creative writing and critical reading are in significant ways the same activity, that better writers make better readers, and better readers, better writers, any way they look at it.

The students also learn that they can talk about literary matters in enjoyable and productive ways—in ways that make even reading and writing a vital part of their personal experience.

11 The Play's the Thing for Middle School Students

Robert W. Blake
State University of New York
College at Brockport

Showing middle school students how to see a play as they read it is my purpose here. Even though I take for granted the inexplicable magic of live theater, I need at the outset to ask myself the following: Why teach kids to read drama? Why take valuable class time to instruct them in reading a play?

First, I know drama is the oldest form of narrative, of storytelling. When I think of "drama," what first comes to mind is something that entertains; I get images of people flocking to Broadway musicals or watching TV shows with cops and robbers or seeing movies with monsters and spaceships. But the ancient Greeks, I know, invented plays not to entertain but to enlighten; their plays were sacred community vehicles for presenting a nonliterate people with acceptable and nonacceptable ways of acting, the codes of behavior for their culture. I realize the Greeks did write comedies, but I also realize they took drama much more seriously than we do now: plays were an integral part of their lives. Although Willy Loman is not, according to Aristotle, a tragic hero, the ancient Greeks would be more at home watching Arthur Miller's *Death of a Salesman* than they would *A Chorus Line*. So a good play—one that people have seen fit to save—embodies implicitly, rather than teaching explicitly—issues which are basic to a culture's survival. These are the real reasons why school youngsters should be taught how to apprehend worthwhile dramatic texts.

If the ways of behaving enacted in plays are so important, though, why not simply state them in an essay or philosophical treatise? Because that's not the way we comprehend in a lasting way. When we see humans on a stage in conflict over profound human matters, we perceive the codes of behavior made flesh and blood, and we remember and learn. Only by reading, discussing, and interpreting

53

a worthwhile play, and then by producing it, will students learn how
to read and see a play by themselves, especially young people who
have no tradition of playgoing.

Why Read This Play? (Rationale)

Generally speaking, students need to learn how to read, interpret,
and present a play simply because drama is a basic human activity.
In specific terms, though, I need to ask myself why they should read
and produce a particular play, W. W. Jacobs' *The Monkey's Paw.* First,
this play is a rousing tale of the supernatural. (Although Stephen
King never gives credit for it, the plot of his novel *Pet Sematary* is
that of *The Monkey's Paw.*) Furthermore, the play is a model of a taut,
well-made dramatic piece with three scenes, a single setting, only five
characters, and every word contributing toward a single preconceived
effect.

The play, however, is more than a macabre potboiler; it deals with
an elemental human issue: the possible existence of fate. Although
at first meeting the characters appear ordinary enough, they represent
various responses to this notion. Herbert, the son, is skeptical of the
power of the monkey's paw. Sergeant-Major Morris, a credible witness,
is one who has observed at firsthand the powers of the occult. Mr.
White, the father, believes in fate if it brings him personal gain. Mrs.
White, the mother, initially uninterested in the men's debates, believes
in unnatural forces the most strongly when they are called upon to
return her son from the dead. This is a tightly constructed play,
then, one which reveals through characters in action various views
toward a supernatural manifestation of fate, with the most satisfying
response to the notion of fate being—in this play, at least—that it is
better not to contest fate but to live one's life ignorant of the unseen
and irrational forces that can be unleashed by our meddling with the
unknown.

Knowledge the Students Will Assimilate and the Skills They Will Practice (General Instructional Objectives)

After having read, discussed, and interpreted a well-made and worthwhile play and presented it orally as either readers theater, acting
with scripts, or actually producing it in the classroom or on stage,
the students will be able to:

- respond emotionally, possibly with personal associations, to a play.
- describe the setting of a play, including its physical location, furniture, and other properties.
- explain what the characters in the play are like, based upon how the playwright describes them and what they say and do.
- tell how characters move around the stage and explain how their movements and personalities relate to the overall meaning of the play.
- describe dramatic elements of plot, initial situation, rising action, climax, and final resolution; tell how these elements are exemplified in a play; and relate their significance to the total impact of the play.
- discuss with the teacher and with other students questions (teacher- or student-created) designed to help comprehend setting, characters, and plot.
- make a statement about the value of a play, based upon intrinsic and extrinsic criteria, with the statement being substantiated by evidence from the play.
- cooperate with other students and adults in producing a play, using one of three approaches: readers theater, acting with scripts, or actual production.

How to Teach the Play (Teaching Strategies)

I need to make a number of professional judgments when I teach the play. If my students are fairly sophisticated about reading and producing plays, then I can review quickly the matters of plot, character development, theme, staging, and so forth. If the students are largely ignorant of these matters—as I suspect most middle school youngsters would be—then it's necessary to spend some time introducing and establishing these notions. In any event, I want to have the students read the play fairly quickly for an initial personal reaction and then read it over a second time more carefully and systematically, after which they will finally produce the play for an audience.

Reading the Play as a Script

To have a firm basis for future reading of plays, students need essentially to read the play as a script. I explain to the students that when a director and actors first read a play as a group, they follow the same procedure. I have the students sit in a circle or move their seats around to form a rectangular table large enough to include everybody. I assign them various parts, showing them as they go along how to read a dramatic text as a script so they might assimilate setting, character, physical appearance, mannerisms, voice, background, motivation, delivery of lines, and the overall pacing and tone of the play.

Setting

To introduce the students to setting, I draw a diagram of a typical proscenium arch stage on the chalkboard and direct them to "set the stage" by drawing in the features of the set, including walls, windows, drapes, and all furniture and other properties and their positions on the stage. Later, I might encourage interested students to draw or paint a picture of the set or to construct a model of the set design.

Characters

I tell the students that they can begin to understand the characters by visualizing what they look like from the playwright's descriptions. For instance, in *The Monkey's Paw*, the author tells us that Mrs. White is "a pleasant-looking woman," but leaves it up to the readers to create their own images of the character.

I learn most about the characters in a play, however, by what they say and do. I need to impress upon the students that from the speeches and behavior of the characters, they can gather evidence to substantiate their responses to the play and justify their interpretations of the play.

Plot

If the students are ignorant of traditional ways of viewing plot, I introduce basic terms dealing with the structure of a play. I may either run off the items with a copy for each student or write them down on the chalkboard and take a few minutes discussing them to make sure we all share generally agreed-upon meanings. I point out that a play, like any other story, has to start at a certain place, move along in a specific direction, and end satisfactorily. It has, in other words, a beginning, middle, and ending, and the parts all fit together—like any work of art—in a satisfying whole.

1. *Initial situation:* The first part of a play introduces the conflict. If the play is short, usually one major character meets a single problem or conflict about which he or she must make a decision. The rest of the play deals with how the major character attempts to resolve the problem and what happens as a result of his or her behavior.

2. *Rising action:* After the playwright has established the major conflict, introduced the characters, and provided the necessary exposition (in the best plays, subtly and unobtrusively), he or she must keep our interest in the play. This is done by introducing a series of complications following from the main character's reaction to the initial conflict.

3. *Climax:* The climax is the high point of the play, the part of greatest intensity. It is the instant at which the chief character decides to act one way or another with respect to the major conflict.

4. *Resolution:* The resolution is what happens to the main character—and to the characters who have reacted to him or her in some way—as a result of how he or she behaved when faced with the major conflict. The technical term for the final resolution in a play is the French word *dénouement*—literally translated as "untying"—which signifies an "unravelling of the plot of a play or novel" (*American Heritage Dictionary* 1973).

Reading Orally, Discussing, and Interpreting the Play

After the students have read the play out loud fairly quickly, I have them reread it in a systematic fashion. At this point, it's a good idea to have them read out loud each of the three scenes separately and discuss the play as a group, following—but certainly not restricted by—the guide questions provided below. Once they have learned how to use teacher-designed questions, they will become confident with framing their own questions as a technique for satisfying for themselves what is happening in a play.

Discussing Scene One

1. What is the setting of the play? Describe the White cottage. How is it furnished, and where are the furnishings placed?

2. What does Mrs. White look like? How does she feel about the men's wishing on the monkey's paw?

3. Describe Mr. White. What do we learn about him from Scene One?

4. Tell us about the Sergeant-Major. (First of all, what is a Sergeant-Major? What kind of a man becomes and remains a Sergeant-Major?) He says he is "tough." How do we know this? Relate the story he tells about the monkey's paw. What is the "essential meaning" of this story to you? State your understanding in a few sentences. Is this an unusual tale to be told by a tough army man? Why?

5. In an effective opening scene, the playwright includes words and events that will crop up later in the play. We call this practice *foreshadowing*. Every word, especially in a short play, counts. Note where the following details occur and, after you have read the whole play, relate their significance to the plot:
   • exactly how much money Mr. White stills owes on the house.
   • Herbert's shift at work. At what time does he usually come home?
   • what kind of job Herbert has.
   • what the first wish on the monkey's paw was.
   • why the old fakir put the curse on the monkey's paw. How the wish would come true "so natural."
   • what the bolt on the front door to the cottage was like.

Discussing Scene Two

1. What does Mr. Sampson look like? What is his purpose in the play?

2. How does the playwright keep our suspense in Scene Two after the initial conflict? What complications arise?

3. How was Herbert killed? How was his killing related to the initial conflict? Did we have a hint—a foreshadowing—in Scene Two of how he was to die? What was it?

Discussing Scene Three

1. How long has it been between Scene Two and Scene Three?

2. Why does Mrs. White, who didn't believe in the monkey's paw, now want to make a wish on it?

3. What foreshadowing do we have that if Herbert is brought back to life, it would not be a good thing?

4. What is the effect of the candle going out—"utter darkness"— as Mrs. White makes her wish?

5. Why didn't Herbert appear immediately when Mrs. White wished for him to be alive?

6. How does the playwright keep the suspense mounting toward the end of Scene Three? Describe in detail how he accomplishes this.

7. Why does Mr. White make the last wish? Explain.

8. What is the effect of the ending of the scene—quiet after "tempestuous" knocking, "a flood of moonlight. Emptiness. The old man sways in prayer on his knees. The old woman lies half swooning, wailing against the door post." Explain in your own words what is happening.

Discussing the Play as a Whole

Now that the students have read the entire play over a second time, the class needs to talk about it as a whole. Questions like the following are designed to encourage general discussion.

1. How did the reading of the play make you feel? Explain your feelings.

2. Did you enjoy the play? Why or why not? Did it hold your interest? If so, how did it do so? Did you wish to know what would happen next once you started reading?

3. Although the basic idea is an incredible one, how did the playwright make the plot seem plausible? Did the complications, for instance, proceed realistically from the initial conflict? Given the way the characters reveal themselves, was the climax appropriate? Was the final resolution—dénouement—satisfying? Did you feel at the ending that this is the way "things should be"?

4. Were the characters believable? In what ways? Was what they said consistent with what they did?

5. What do you suppose the playwright is saying about people and life in general? (You might wish to think about the friendly dispute between Herbert and the Sergeant-Major in Scene One.)

6. How good was the play? There are two ways of judging the play. First, how well was it put together? And second, does the play deal with something important for people to think about? Support your evaluation with evidence from the text.

Putting on the Play

Now that the students have read the play out loud quickly for a general impression and have reread it more carefully, following systematic strategies, they will find it rewarding to produce the play in one of three ways:

Readers theater: The actors sit on stools before an audience in class or on a stage and read from their scripts held in binders.

Acting with scripts: The actors walk through the play with scripts in their hands before an audience in class or on a stage.

Actual production: The actors produce the play before an audience in class or on stage. The actors memorize their lines, use expressive gestures, move about the stage, wear costumes, and use properties, such as furniture and other objects.

If the students stage an actual production, they need to decide about the following:

1. Setting: Should there be flats to designate the White house or should there be just curtains and the necessary furniture and other properties?
2. Lighting: How would lighting and other special effects be used?
3. Parts: Which students would be best suited for the roles? Students who wish to play certain parts should read or try out. It may be advisable to have more than one cast for the play, to give more students practice in acting.
4. Makeup: How should the characters appear? What makeup is needed?
5. Costuming: What costumes are necessary?
6. Properties: What furniture and other properties should be rounded up?
7. Acting: The students need to learn the fundamentals of acting on a stage:
   - how to move across a stage, move upstage, and move downstage
   - how to assume stage positions
   - how to memorize lines
   - how to reflect emotions
   - how to make stage gestures
   - how to play a character realistically, such as an old lady or a military man
   - how to achieve and vary pace

Evaluation

My evaluation techniques are directly related to my purpose—teaching middle school students to see a play as they read it. Moreover,

I can use my general instructional objectives directly for evaluating the students' success.

The following are various ways of assessing how well the students have learned the terms related to dramatic literature and how well they can perform the skills necessary for reading, responding, and interpreting plays. Students will:

1. Make an immediate emotional response to a play (short written response).

2. Describe or define, with examples,
   • the general elements of setting, plot, characters, and theme.
   • dramatic elements of a play, such as initial situation, rising action, climax, and final resolution.
   • the three kinds of play production (readers theater, acting with scripts, and actual production).
   • the basic elements of play production, such as setting, lighting, acting, makeup, properties, and costuming (oral recitation or short written responses).

3. Explain how the general elements of a play and the dramatic elements of a play are exemplified in a particular play (oral recitation or short written responses).

4. Describe how a particular play could be adapted to various methods of production (oral recitation or short written responses).

5. Describe how the elements of play production—setting, lighting, acting, makeup, properties, costuming—are demonstrated in a particular play (oral recitation or short written responses).

6. Identify the elements of a play and analyze how the elements are employed by the playwright in a particular play (oral recitation or short written responses).

7. Make a statement about the value of a play, using intrinsic criteria (e.g., how well the structure of a particular play holds together) and extrinsic criteria (e.g., how valuable and valid are the notions revealed in the play about how human beings behave) (written response).

8. Read a play they have not read or seen and write a response to the play, including the following:
   • a personal emotional reaction
   • an analysis of the general elements and dramatic elements of the play and of how the playwright has exemplified them

- a personal statement of the value of the play, basing this evaluation upon intrinsic and extrinsic criteria and upon substantiation from the text

Where Do We Go from Here?

My middle school students have learned a basic vocabulary for dealing with dramatic texts, have learned by producing a short, well-made play how the elements of dramatic literature work to produce a single powerful effect, and have learned how to use systematic strategies for reading, responding, and interpreting new plays. They are now ready—as they mature socially and psychologically—to apply their internalized understanding of dramaturgy and play production to more challenging full-length plays such as *Our Town* and *Death of a Salesman,* and with the expert guidance of a sensitive and knowledgeable teacher to turn to the great dramatic texts of Western civilization, *Hamlet* and *Antigone.* If I have been successful with my planning and instruction, they are well prepared for this most basic and crucial of human endeavors.

References

American Heritage Dictionary of the English Language. 1973. Boston: Houghton Mifflin.

Jacobs, W. W. 1910. The Monkey's Paw. In *Thirty Famous One-Act Plays,* edited by Bennett Cerf and Van H. Cartmell. 1943. New York: The Modern Library.

12 Spoken Literature in the English Classroom

Jonathan R. Eller, Major, USAF, and
Dennis C. Porter, Major, USAF
U.S. Air Force Academy

> I flunked Oral Expression. . . . It's this course where each boy in class has to get up in class and make a speech. You know. Spontaneous and all. And if the boy digresses at all, you're supposed to yell "Digression!" at him as fast as you can. It just about drove me crazy. I got an *F* in it.[1]

Holden Caulfield's description of an absurdly impersonal speech class has brought a chuckle to two generations of teachers. We laugh because we know that J. D. Salinger's self-appointed catcher in the rye would never have such an inhumane experience in our own classrooms. Nevertheless, Holden's fictional experience reminds us of a very real teaching challenge: to give our students a personal and stimulating context for the rhetorical principles we teach. A time-tested way to do this is to read and write about literature. But reading and writing aren't the only ways to apprehend literature; in fact, there is a vast body of literature (now often relegated to other departments) which was meant to be spoken and heard. This literature—the oral tradition of drama and oratory—can be used in any English course to develop speaking and listening abilities. Oral literature not only integrates the development of speaking and listening skills but also prepares students for more advanced literature courses in the upper-division curriculum.

The study of oral literature is an ancient practice which still has a place in the classroom. Speech teachers since Quintilian's time have known that the study of real examples of the best public discourse can bring textbook generalizations to life in the classroom. This

---

1. Salinger, J. D. *The Catcher in the Rye.* (1951; New York: Bantam, 1964), p. 183. All further references to this work appear in the text.

premise has a long-standing corollary in composition theory, as evidenced by the great number of composition readers and anthologies in use today. But if we can use literature to teach writing skills, we can use it to develop speaking and listening skills as well. English teachers who can use dramatic literature and great speeches together in the classroom will have little trouble convincing students that speaking and listening skills are inextricably linked, and that these skills can be simultaneously developed.

Our paradigm for discussion is the sophomore English course at the United States Air Force Academy. In this course, we use oral literature to teach speech and writing and to promote a better understanding of the literature.

Drama

We begin with four lessons on *Julius Caesar*—a play which contains some of the greatest rhetorical speeches in the English language. And, since great things are at stake in the lives of every character, we have the opportunity to develop both performance techniques and values debate through one work of literature.

We combine analysis and performance in classroom activities which lead up to graded oral and written presentations at the end of the study block. We begin with impromptu exercises based on the themes and issues of *Julius Caesar*. The impromptus form a bridge between the act of reading the play and actual literary analysis. Topics include the power of speech, the use and abuse of power, ambition, the role of women in the play, one-man rule versus democracy, friendship, and suicide as an ethical response to failure. Each impromptu topic is phrased in such a way that the topic opens up for the student speaker. Here are some sample topics:

> The Power of Speech: How do speeches influence actions in the play? Which are the most vivid examples of the power of speech?
>
> Friendship: How far should one go in honoring one's obligations to friends? Are the duties required of friendship invoked properly or improperly in the play?

The students have one minute to organize and two minutes to deliver a response to the topic. In these "blitzkrieg" reviews, we force the students to think on their feet not only about speaking but about the themes, characters, and events of the drama. The impromptu activity enhances their confidence in speaking about literature and gives them a chance to speak under pressure before they have to do it for a grade.

Next, we work with direct quotations from the play. Students deliver a passage and then establish the thematic and structural significance of it. For instance, we direct them to Brutus's key statement on honor in Act I: "Set honor in one eye and death i' th' other, / And I will look on both indifferently; / For let the gods so speed me, as I love / The name of honor more than I fear death."[2] A student will deliver the quotation in character and then step outside the role of Brutus to comment on the literary significance of the passage. Delivery helps students hear the rhythm and significance of the language and, on a practical level, aids in their understanding of Elizabethan English. Commenting on the significance of the passage reinforces the earlier impromptu exercise and ties language to theme and content.

So far, we've stayed away from the two great speeches of the play—the funeral orations of Brutus and Antony. That's because we want the students to first understand what the play is about, and we want them to become familiar with Shakespeare's language. The pattern of exercises so far, then, has built toward student role-playing of the crucial funeral scene. Now students will stand before their peers and act the roles for the audience. One player can handle the brief orations by Brutus, but we break Antony's oration into four parts. These five "players" work to an active audience which has in effect become the plebeians and the mob. The deliveries are not continuous—rather, there is a break between each player's performance to critique both delivery and effectiveness. The entire class, already involved in the action of the scene, is certainly in the mood to offer substantive comments on the success of each speaker's interpretive strategy. The players must do exactly what Shakespeare intended *his* players to do—persuade an audience to believe and to act.

With this series of exercises, students develop an appreciation for the power of speech which will take them through the final two acts of *Julius Caesar.* We conclude our study of the play with a capstone dramatic exercise—confrontation and interaction between characters. Students interpret the exchange between Antony and Octavius in Rome (IV.i.1–51), the confrontation between Brutus and Cassius at Sardis (IV.iii.1–122), and the final parley between Antony, Octavius,

---

2. Shakespeare, William. *Julius Caesar,* ed. William and Barbara Rosen (New York: New American Library, 1963), I.ii.86–89. All further references to this work are keyed to this edition and appear in the text.

Brutus, and Cassius at Philippi (V.i.1–125). The audience feedback on delivery leads naturally into a final discussion of the quality of persuasion evident in the text itself.

Oratory

We follow *Julius Caesar* with several pieces from another tradition of spoken literature—oratory. Since we have been studying drama about revolutionaries and the power of speech, we move on to historical speeches by revolutionaries such as Lenin, Malcolm X, Patrick Henry, and John Hancock. Students read the speeches and in some instances see actual videotapes of the speakers. We use student impromptus and oral interpretations to analyze the technique and content of these speeches. Oratory will be far less familiar to the English student— the challenge here is to listen carefully to the oral interpretations and videos in an effort to apprehend the dominant arguments and strategies of the speeches. Seeing the delivery adds a crucial dimension to this activity: as students see Malcolm X speaking or hear a classmate's interpretation of one of Patrick Henry's powerful ad- dresses, they learn through the enactment.

Oral interpretations and videos carry over to the study of traditional literary genres as well. The essay, perhaps the easiest form to analyze in terms of rhetorical principles, lends itself especially well to oral interpretation. Students can see selected cuts from Jacob Bronowski's "The Ascent of Man" or perhaps deliver some of his well-known essays such as "The Creative Mind" or "The Reach of the Imagi- nation." Fiction includes segments tailor-made for oral delivery. "The Grand Inquisitor" chapter of *The Brothers Karamazov* is often extracted for anthologies and naturally lends itself to oral interpretation. There are many other accessible extracts: Huxley's chilling account of the London Hatchery in the first chapter of *Brave New World,* Dalton Trumbo's graphic description of the "living dead" in chapter five of *Johnny Got His Gun,* and of course the self-contained episodes from Mark Twain's *Roughing It* and *Life on the Mississippi.*

Poetry, an oral literary genre we normally teach in an English class, has unlimited possibilities for oral interpretation. Once again, we want the speaker to develop the ability to interpret and persuade through the literary selection, and we want the audience to provide active feedback: in a very real sense, initial audience reaction is an oral "reaction paper" to both the content of the literature and the speaker's delivery of the literature. And since literature is the focus, the speaker will feel less threatened. On this point we've taken a lesson from contemporary speech theory, which emphasizes shared experience and shared meaning between speaker and audience rather than the kind of antagonistic relationship which Holden Caulfield encounters in the "Digression" exercise. Unlike the students in Holden's class, our students aren't held responsible for authorship of the content, but only for interpretations—some dramatic, some analytical—of the content. Therefore, the performers and the student listeners can discover the spoken qualities and dynamics of literature in a social context which minimizes the distractions inherent in public speaking.

Conclusion

In the exercises described above, all of the students are players. Each one has a stake in studying literature based on a group requirement to interact—a requirement which often blossoms into a personal commitment to understand the values inherent in a work of literature. The exercises give students nonthreatening opportunities to experience the spoken qualities of literature, and to use what they hear, see, and read in the analysis of literary works. Discussions become more meaningful, allowing the students a better opportunity to make connections between literature and their own lives. When speaking and listening exercises become part of the literary experience, students cannot fail to develop confidence and ability as speakers and listeners.

Holden Caulfield is a frustrated student because the "Oral Expression" class activities prohibit him from developing a personal context for his studies. Speech should be a way to bring interest into the classroom, but it isn't. Holden makes the plea himself:

> What I think is, you're supposed to leave somebody alone if he's at least being interesting and he's getting all excited about something. I like it when somebody gets excited about something. It's nice. (pp. 184–85)

We've designed exercises which develop cognitive and rhetorical abilities by letting students discover and express individual interests in the literature. Almost any literature we teach will have a spoken quality we can use to generate this kind of interest. And, as Holden says, that's nice.

13 A Speaking Project about the Arts That Acknowledges Students' Underlife

Hallie S. Lemon
Western Illinois University

In discussing "The Underlife and Writing Instruction," Robert Brooke (1987) asserts that writing teachers encourage our students to see themselves as original thinkers. Our pedagogy goes "beyond the roles offered by the normal teacher-as-lecturer, student-as-passive-learner education system" (p. 141). Successful strategies from our writing classes, such as collaborative projects and students' own choice of topics, can be adapted for speaking activities involving the arts to encourage students to be critical thinkers as well.

Too often we ask our classes to evaluate works of art that we love or that are a part of accepted anthologies, and we wonder why the students have little to say. Why not give them an opportunity to speak about the art forms they're already appreciating? To completely reverse the roles, whether in a literature course or composition course, why not let the students teach us? For the collaborative speaking project described here, I ask groups to lead a class discussion on a work or works of their choice. I have discovered that students can articulate complex insights and teach me to understand their favorite art forms.

To be successful, this undertaking needs some grounding in the terminology of criticism but could be used as a starting point to lead students from what they know and like to an appreciation of other forms of literature and art. In my class, however, we have already studied critical reading, research techniques, a novel, and chapters on critiquing the arts. Early in the semester I first mention the project by telling the students that they will be able to determine what the class studies on the final assignment and, therefore, that they should start thinking of possible works. I encourage them to talk to each other to probe common interests. Then, as sign-up time nears, past successes and possibilities for future topics are flashed at them daily. Always the focus is on what the students are actually reading, watching, or hearing: "What do you like? Are you arranging your class schedules so you don't miss your favorite soap opera? Let's take a close look at that soap opera. Are the characters realistic? The plots? What new insights will we discover when we take this closer look?"

Successful topics for this project have included soap operas (popular with as many males as females), one-act plays such as Edward Albee's *The Sandbox*, television series of all types, comparison of stereotyped roles on various television series, short stories, song lyrics, a sculpture exhibit, family roles in television series (especially as they have changed over the years), cartoon characters, comparison of styles in two comic monologues, a seminar on jazz, individual movies, and the hero figure in a current series of movies. With the availability of VCRs and tape recorders in most schools, the possibilities are almost endless.

What's more, I find the students to be more familiar with these audiovisual forms than I am. Rather than employing them as an aid to the printed word, the students have been viewing these forms *instead* of the printed word. At the 1987 Wyoming Conference on English, which focused on literacy, Shirley Brice Heath said that one thing we might do to improve the cultural literacy of our youth is to use television as a book, and talk about what we watch with our children. This speaking project asks the students to talk about works they already know and enjoy; in so doing, they learn criteria for evaluating other works which might be enjoyed if better known.

For this assignment, the students, in groups of three or four depending on the size and length of the class, take over the entire class period, make the assignments, present the background, and lead the discussion of their creative work(s). About a month before the presentations begin, the students sign up for their day and topic. I usually give extra credit to the group that volunteers to present first, and I invite open comments on that initial presentation; therefore, that beginning day is most often the first one signed up for. This signing up for topics and groups is sometimes the hardest part of the entire project; I try to foster some variety in each class—only one presentation on a soap opera, no more than two on rock lyrics, etc. Also, one or two students might be left over; however, once they've been taken into a project and gotten started, they will become productive group members. Last semester, four "left-overs" formed one group, changed their topic several times, finally settled on cartoon characters, and gave the most innovative presentation in their class.

Scheduling at least one formal conference for each group and being available for many informal sessions on audiovisual material and such, I also present some of my own favorites as a sample lesson.

In past years, I've enjoyed comparing John Donne's "Meditation 17" with Paul Simon's "I Am a Rock." This year I compared Simon's "I Am a Rock" with his newer "Graceland." While presenting this lesson, I step out of my role as a teacher to comment on how the lesson is going: "Now, that question didn't get much of a response. What could I do now? What other teaching techniques would be effective in presenting this song?"

The students also have a worksheet to help them plan. The worksheet includes a review of the points to consider in the works (character, dialogue, images, etc.), elements to be covered in the conference (class assignments, dittos, audiovisual materials, timing, class management, etc.), and the standards used in evaluation (see below). Each group is given up to five minutes of the previous session to present their assignment to the class.

On the day of the actual presentation, I move to the back of the room and let the students arrange the class the way they think would be most effective. Sometimes they take turns standing behind the podium; sometimes they turn three or four desks around to face the class and speak from these desks. Every once in a while, they even take the class to the theater, art gallery, or music room. A few groups have rearranged the class into a large circle, of which they form a part.

For evaluation I use a large sheet covering the following points, and I jot down comments to the group as they are giving their presentation.

1. *Preparation* includes thought given to the materials in the presentation, time spent in gathering background information, and effective use of any audiovisual material.

2. *Overall Content* includes the way the material is organized, the effectiveness of the introduction and conclusion, and the discussion of specific details in the works.

3. *Presentation* covers the actual presentation of ideas, voice level, eye contact, distraction, and class management.

The students know that these are the main points of evaluation because they are included on the planning worksheet. Once I've recorded the group's grade, I hand the comment sheet to the group for discussion, usually pointing out the main strength and main weakness. On the first day, we leave a little time to talk about that evaluation with the class—good features first, and then what other groups could do even better.

My original intentions in assigning this project were to have my students develop a critical awareness of their own art forms, to recognize what was good and bad, to learn to see the various levels of meaning in any creative work, and to communicate these insights to others. I was surprised by how many were already doing this analysis and could communicate what they perceived remarkably well. On the other hand, I would often find a large grin on my face as one of my "quiet ones" expressed a complex insight more effectively than he or she had done all year.

Of course, no teacher could engineer the way some sessions succeed. The class discussion of a lyric by Prince from *Sign O' the Times* about a woman who killed her baby because she couldn't afford to feed it occurred the day after a student at our school had left her newborn girl in a garbage can. Three students who wanted to show the relationship between the "M*A*S*H" television series and the Vietnam War were late to class only because they were getting into their costumes, which included the uniform of one boy's uncle who had been killed in Vietnam. And the very first time I tried this assignment, four of five members in one of our school's jazz bands were in one class and presented a session on changes in jazz forms. A fellow class member stopped after class to tell me that it was the best class session he'd attended that year.

My prediction is that different but equally memorable occasions will result as you try this project with your classes. In turning the traditional classroom roles around, you will encourage a more conscious awareness of the art forms your students are already appreciating, and you will strengthen their abilities to express their awareness. As Brooke would say, this assignment asks students "to stand apart from the roles they normally play. . . . [and] see themselves . . . as real thinkers with power and ability" (pp. 151–52).

Reference

Brooke, R. 1987. The Underlife and Writing Instruction. *College Composition and Communication* 38: 141–53.

II Talking to Develop Self-Confidence in Communication

14 Strategies for Developing Effective Use of the Voice

Carole Schulte Johnson
Washington State University

Effective use of one's voice is important not only in speaking but also for indicating understanding of literature through performance. Yet during the elementary grades voice development seems to be left to chance. Perhaps this is because the voice strategies suggested in basal reader and language arts series generally are limited. A recent study (Johnson and Gaskins 1986) reported that both types of series had little variety in their voice activities and included only minimal material for practice. Frequently the basals' suggestions were generalizations such as "read with expression" or "show how the character feels by the way you read." These directions are not particularly helpful in understanding *what to do with the voice* in order to perform the activities.

Through the activities described below the voice strategies of pitch, stress, pause, tempo, and emotional expression are used. Visual aspects, such as the arrow cards which are described later, are included when possible. The directions attempt to keep everyone involved; while one individual is using the strategy, listeners are responsible for responding via discussion, writing, or use of cards. Students in upper elementary and junior high grades have used the activities successfully, reporting they not only learned a lot but enjoyed them.

Once the strategies have been introduced, attention to transferring their use to other situations is needed. Transfer can be encouraged by incorporating discussions of possible voice strategies into lessons involving speaking or oral reading. Such discussions usually can be incorporated in the giving of the assignment and/or the introduction to a lesson. Since speaking often involves the development of the material to be spoken, some students will find it easier to transfer the strategies first through the performance of literature. However, it is important that students understand that the same voice strategies can be used effectively in both situations.

75

Pitch, Stress, and Emotion

"Up or Down"

Materials are one arrow card (a 3 × 5 or smaller card with an arrow on it) per player and cards with words, phrases, or short sentences on them. Each word card has a double: the first card has an up arrow following its word(s), while its double has a down arrow. Players take turns drawing a card and reading it with the pitch indicated by the direction of the arrow. Listeners identify the direction of the voice by showing their arrow card in an up or down position.

Sample Cards

Well	Take it easy
Okay	All right
Go	Don't do that
Hey, you	I love it
Let go	Pick it up

"What Word Is It?"

Each card in this pack of cards has the same sentence written on it twice, but with a different word underlined. Each player draws a card and reads the sentence both ways, stressing the underlined word as indicated. Listeners discuss what was stressed in each, and which, if either, they preferred. They can also present additional interpretations of the sentence. A variation is to have the sentences on a worksheet: the listeners respond by underlining the stressed word(s).

Sample Cards

I'm going to talk to you.
I'm going to *talk* to you.
That's not my trouble.
That's *not* my trouble.
The *cat* was huge.
The cat was *huge.*
We ate the *whole* pie.
We *ate* the whole pie.

"What's It Mean?"

Each card has a saying with a list of ways to express the saying. A player picks a card and reads the saying each way. Listeners identify the types of expression/emotion which were voiced. One variation is to have everyone see the drawn card. Then the speaker decides which emotion to express and listeners identify it.

Sample Cards

Hello	a. I'm glad to see you.
	b. I'm sad.
	c. I'm tired.
How are you	a. I'm really interested in you.
	b. I don't really care.
	c. I'm in a hurry.
Really	a. I'm bored.
	b. I want to hear more.
	c. I don't believe it.
How terrible	a. Who cares?
	b. I really mean it.
	c. How sad.
Good morning	a. It's a great day.
	b. I'm grumpy this morning.
	c. I'm surprised, I didn't expect to see you.
I'll see you later	a. I could care less.
	b. I really want to.
	c. You're in trouble.

Pause and Tempo

"Where Are the Stops?"

This activity was developed for use by pairs so that everyone practices the strategy and also responds to its use. Every player has a paper with sentences on it. There are two forms with the same series of sentences on each. On one form, the first half of the sentences has punctuation while the second half does not. The second form has the same sentence order but with reverse punctuation.

One player reads a sentence with punctuation while his or her partner reads the unpunctuated sentence and marks with a slash where a stop or pause is heard. (If the partner prefers, sentences can be read twice—once for listening and once for marking.) Participants can alternate reading and listening, or one can read all of his or her sentences with punctuation first and then reverse roles.

A simpler variation has only unpunctuated sentences on a form. The punctuated version is on a second form or on cards. One person does all the reading of the punctuated form, or if cards are used they can be passed around so all may participate in practicing the strategy.

Sample Sentences for One Form

A. Sentences to be read. (These sentences will not have punctuation on the second form.)

John, Mary, Ellen, and Mark will be playing.

"Beautiful," said the Princess. Her dark eyes were shining.

"Can you believe that happened?" he asked. "Karl, the mouse, chased the cat!"

"Do you want to go, John?" asked Julie. "We're going to the movie."

B. Sentences to be marked with slashes. (On the other form these sentences will have punctuation.)

Many crocodiles live in the rivers and swamps in Africa the swamps and rivers are full of leeches.

Once upon a time two soldiers were walking along a country road they had just returned from leave in a big city.

Look at that man said Joe he is green.

How are you today Sue asked John you look great.

"On Curves or Straightaway"

The teacher or student prepares and reads a selection of short poems, parts of poems, and/or lines from stories which lend themselves to having some part(s) speeded up and/or slowed down. Listeners have a card with a straight line (to indicate speeding up) on one side and a curve (to indicate slowing down) on the other. They show the curve or straightaway when appropriate, leaving the card flat for normal speed. For variation listeners can pair up and see if they agree with each other.

Combinations

"Doing It All"

Either cards or a paper with a variety of sentences and paragraphs can be used. (Children's literature and poetry provide good sources.)

After a quick review of the voice strategies, each player prepares and then presents. His or her partner or the rest of the group act as the editing group, discussing the strategies used, what they liked about the presentation, how else it could have been done, and what might have improved it.

Sample Selections

"You better get out of here, you dumb dog, before you get in more trouble," Martin shouted. "Go on, Gus, go home!" (*Martin by Himself*, Skurzynski 1979)

"Are you taking your teddy bear along?"
"Taking my teddy bear along!" I said.
"To my friend's house? Are you kidding?
That's the silliest thing I ever heard!
Of course, I'm not taking my teddy bear."
(*Ira Sleeps Over*, Waber 1972)

Should I take him?
"Take him," said my mother.
"Take him," said my father.
"But Reggie will laugh," I said.
"He'll say I'm a baby."
"He won't laugh," said my mother.
"He won't laugh," said my father.
"He'll laugh," said my sister. (*Ira Sleeps Over*, Waber 1972)

Finally Jill went to see Gwen.
"I'm sorry for all the things I said."
"It's O.K.," said Gwen. "I knew you were upset. How's the baseball coming?"
"Awful," said Jill. "I've been in a real slump. Tomorrow's the first game, and I bet I'm not in the lineup." (*Something Queer at the Ball Park*, Levy 1975)

King Pilaf of Mulligatawny was having a very bad day. To begin with he bumped his head against the Lord Chamberlain's upon getting out of bed. Then he discovered a hole in the heel of his stockings that was the size of a marble. And he knew without asking that his breakfast gingerbread would be crumbly again. (*The Queen Who Couldn't Bake Gingerbread*, Van Woerkom 1975)

Until one day, when everything went wrong. The King dropped the crown on his foot, and the Queen awoke with a headache. The Lord Chamberlain was ill, and the cook slept late. The court painter put his head through the Majesties' new portrait, and the Queen's dog chewed up all the paintbrushes. Outside, it snowed one minute and rained the next. (*The Queen Who Couldn't Bake Gingerbread*, Van Woerkom 1975)

"Self Selection"

At this point students are ready to choose their own materials to practice the effective use of their voice. They often enjoy working in small groups and presenting to the rest of the class or other classrooms. Such presentations also reinforce the incorporation of the strategies into their regular speaking and interpretation of literature.

References

Johnson, C. S., and J. Gaskins. 1986. Enriching Reading through the Teaching of Oral Reading. Paper presented at the Reading Research Conference of the Washington Organization for Reading Development, Seattle.

Levy, E. 1975. *Something Queer at the Ball Park.* Illus. M. Gerstein. New York: Delacorte.

Skurzynski, G. 1979. *Martin by Himself.* Illus. L. Munsinger. Boston: Houghton Mifflin.

Van Woerkom, D. 1975. *The Queen Who Couldn't Bake Gingerbread.* Illus. P. Galdone. New York: Alfred A. Knopf.

Waber, B. 1972. *Ira Sleeps Over.* Boston: Houghton Mifflin.

15 The Process of Persuasion: An Approach to Thinking, Writing, and Speaking

Dorothy E. Hardin
Hereford High School
Parkton, Maryland

A persuasive composition is like a segment on "60 Minutes." Each segment—compiled, written, and edited for maximum effectiveness—is designed to interest and raise the consciousness of a television audience burned out by more than six hours of football. Although many students may understand this process of persuasion on a TV program, even the best and brightest ignore its implications for their own writing and speaking in English class.

The 1983 National Committee on Excellence in Education report, *A Nation at Risk*, addresses some of the problems with persuasion: "Many 17-year-olds do not possess the higher order intellectual skills we should expect of them," and "only one-fifth can write a persuasive essay." It may seem contradictory, but students in a Gifted and Talented (G/T) program are not automatically gifted and talented thinkers, writers, or speakers. With my group of academically proficient G/T students who comprised the top 4 percent of their junior class, this certainly was the case.

I found that G/T students frequently prefer to write only one draft of anything and sometimes even view themselves as being beyond revision. Therefore, if I could motivate my G/T students to think more critically and care about their persuasive thesis through multiple revisions and an oral presentation, I might gain some insights which could be relevant to students of any ability level or in any discipline.

Through trial and error, I learned to adjust my own approach to persuasive writing and speaking. Finally, I tested my strategies in a process which emphasized focused prewriting, revision, responding, and journal/sourcebook activities, and which stretched intermittently over five weeks while other unit material was being taught. This process culminated in my G/T English II group writing and delivering

effective persuasive speeches to my Honors English II students. As
it turned out, building another group into the process had a significant
impact.

Preparation

In their unit on Ralph Waldo Emerson, G/T English II students are
required to compose and present a persuasive speech featuring some
of Emerson's rhetorical devices. Without telling the students that
they would be required to write their own speeches, I involved them
in a series of motivational prewriting activities. Before assigning
Emerson's "The American Scholar" speech, I asked them to react
to a Think Sheet, which listed six statements designed to promote
critical thinking. "The first in time and the first in importance of
the influences upon the mind is that of nature" is one of six key
Emerson quotes adjusted for use on the Think Sheet, as shown in
this excerpt:

STATEMENTS	I THINK . . .	THE AUTHOR SAID . . .
1. The most important influence upon the mind is TV.		

Before reading, the students jotted down their responses on the "I
THINK" portion. A basis for discussion, the statements and responses
also enabled students to locate more quickly the main ideas in
Emerson's turgid transcendental prose.

During the Think Sheet activity, students confronted some of the
basic issues of the roles of nature and the scholar in early nineteenth-
century American society. This led to a review of Emerson's use of
rhetorical devices, some of which they would need to employ in their
own speeches.

As a more contemporary example of persuasive composition,
William Faulkner's Nobel Prize acceptance speech was assigned.
However, the students handled the discussion of an additional Think
Sheet before and after the reading in a seminar setting. As a
contributor and resource person, I guided the class toward a comparison of the persuasive approaches used by Emerson and Faulkner
and the audiences to which each writer aimed his ideas.

Finally, I broke the news that they would have to write a persuasive speech and present it to my first-period Honors English II students, a group whose academic standing placed them within the top 10 percent of the same junior class. Therefore, the ultimate audience was not the teacher. Suddenly, it was not just another assignment for my G/T students. There was something extra riding on this one: their reputations. Peer pressure can be a wonderful thing.

Knowing that the students would have some difficulty in finding the right topic, I provided them with a Brainstorm Sheet, essentially a blank sheet with concept organizers placed on it. They jotted down responses to the following categories on the Brainstorm Sheet: audience, topics/things I feel strongly about (love/hate), topic I can support the most effectively in a persuasive speech, content details I can use to persuade audience (major/minor supports), and writing techniques I can use to persuade the audience. Next, I had the students break into small groups to discuss the generated topics and ideas.

At this stage, final topic problems were resolved by the whole class. It was evident that I was evolving into a consultant and a collaborator in the persuasive process and had shed my guises of authority figure and "giver of the grade." For example, these intelligent and glib students asked me to work at least two library periods into the following week's planning schedule. They knew their Honors peers would expect specific evidence from authoritative sources to add credibility to the persuasive speeches. Susan, whose topic was book banning and censorship, wanted to interview one of the school librarians for possible instances of censorship in her high school, county, and state. This would make the speech more meaningful to her local teenage audience.

At this point in the process, the students and I go over a specification sheet for evaluating the written assignment. Using a G/T student's first draft from the previous year as a composition model, I show how the sheet is used as a revision tool. The sheet is essentially a set of objectives covering the introduction, body, and conclusion of the composition. For example, the body of the piece "shall have effective use of rhetorical questions, . . . effective use of clear imagery, . . . and the use of personal pronouns to appeal to the audience." Together we redesign the sheet for use in evaluating this year's compositions.

Within the week, the students analyzed their own first-draft speeches for strengths and weaknesses in peer response groups. Joining one of the groups, I heard Susan complete the reading of her speech. Sharing the opinion that her introduction was weak, the students suggested more "life" and audience involvement. As one student said, "You don't want to put them to sleep in the first 30 seconds."

All students produced multiple drafts, each one showing more focus in content and growth in personal style. Since they knew another class would be listening to the speeches, they became increasingly conscious of the necessity for rewriting. Moreover, the raised consciousness about revision carried over into other assignments throughout the rest of the year, revealing their breakthrough belief in its value.

I asked students to comment in a sourcebook/learning log entry on their speeches in the "final draft stage." Susan wrote,

> I found that each draft I did improved a lot over the previous one so that now my final draft is greatly improved over my original draft. I'm especially glad that I was able to come up with an effective opening and rhetorical questions. . . . While I was writing the speech, I think I actually further convinced myself about censorship.*

Similar comments from other students in the class revealed their increased confidence as a result of revising and thinking about their topics. However, other sourcebook entries provided a key to the next stage of the persuasive process. Jeff wrote, "I feel very insecure. I really don't have much confidence speaking to others."

In a class discussion, the students brainstormed effective speech delivery techniques. Items such as voice level, eye contact, gestures or body language, dramatic phrasing, and independence from manuscript were included on a response sheet used to help students improve the delivery of their speeches—an obvious area of concern for all of them. The "P-Q-P" response areas were *praise* for the speaker, *questions* for the speaker, and what the speaker should *polish*. After a week of oral preparation on their own, the students presented their five-minute speeches on two scheduled days in the classroom. Each student and I completed a P-Q-P sheet for each speaker.

On the third day, we discussed our feelings about the speeches and the elements which still needed work before their final presentations to the Honors English II class. The praise comments were very supportive for even the weakest speaker. Questions were related to a variety of areas, such as pronunciation, weak conclusions, and content specifics. Although the praise and question comments sometimes still referred to content, all of the polish comments addressed

---

* Note: All of the student writing samples used in this article are quoted exactly as they were written; however, student names were changed.

the speech delivery very specifically. Typical comments were "Need a little more practice reading it aloud to make it more clear," "Look at your audience—don't shut us out," "Try not to laugh," "Slow down a little (machine-gun delivery at times)," and "Articulate more clearly."

While some students were ready to deliver their speeches, others were not. I agreed to coach these students, and their classmates also offered help. A supportive atmosphere pervaded the group, which now included me, the teacher with whom they used to play that old game, grade roulette. Thus, their greatest anxiety was not the effect the assignment would have on their grade-point averages; it was peer fear.

Performance

The speakers went to the period-one Honors English II class in pairs. They were directed to respond in sourcebook entries to feelings about their own speech delivery, the delivery of their partner, and the attitudes/reactions of the period-one class. Moreover, I asked the Honors students to react to the speeches and speakers in their sourcebooks. The sourcebook responses and the results of class discussions about the experience accentuated the success of the assignment and brought to the surface some surprises. For example, Bill, whose speech confronted the issue of too much sexuality in the media, wrote the following:

> When talking to students later about my speech they all said they liked it, but that may have been just to make me feel better (not that I mind). I believe the class felt all of our speeches were good and respected the time and effort we put into them.

This theme of hard work and the rewards of revision and practice was evident in a majority of the G/T sourcebook entries.

The only direction given to the Honors students was to treat the speakers as they themselves would wish to be treated. Their behavior and attitude were complimented by the G/T students consistently. Tom, whose speech attacked TV evangelists, titled his sourcebook entry "First Period: Are There Group Rates for Heaven?" He wrote:

> Absolutely amazing. Studious. Quiet. Attentive. Supportive. Believe it or not, all of these adjectives describe your first period class. They were great. . . . The next amazing thing about your class is that they think. Maybe you don't think that is such a big deal but I know it is. I could not imagine spending 1st period Monday morning listening to a bunch of G/T speeches. (I would

think—"Yeah, a chance to sleep!") Instead, your first period
students actually discussed the topic after the speech was over.

I, too, was impressed with the thinking being done by my Honors
students.

Sitting at the rear of the room, I observed my students becoming
the teacher. I became merely another student. And what I was
learning related not so much to the speeches as to the interaction
occurring among the students. Things were happening that I had
not expected, and those things were very positive. The sourcebook
responses from the Honors class validated these observations.

The assignment of a persuasive speech filled with Emersonian
rhetorical devices had evolved into something more complex. Laurie's
comments typified the reactions of her entire Honors class:

> When the G/T students started to give their speeches, I must
> admit, I felt a little apprehensive. As bad as it may sound, I like
> many others often feel put off by these students who have been
> placed in a class more advanced than ours. I wasn't sure if I
> would like the idea of them speaking to our class. . . . Although
> some dealt with topics of war . . . the topics of Tele-Evangelism,
> book banning, . . . actually had me laughing. It gave us a chance
> to see these students, who we felt were too in depth for us, in
> a different light.

Transcending its original purpose, the speech assignment had culminated in some attitude adjustments among students in both classes.

My Gifted and Talented students had persuaded their Honors
peers about more than their topics. The social angle was the most
interesting outgrowth of this experience. In a classroom situation,
two groups of students and a teacher had the opportunity to speak,
interact, and learn from and about one another. I learned that the
process approach does not relate only to composition. The persuasive
process can lead to social insights which are far more valuable than
written words alone.

Bibliography

McTighe, Jay. 1985. Teaching for Thinking, of Thinking, and about
    Thinking. *School* 3 (June): 1–6.
Murray, Donald M. 1984. *Write to Learn.* New York: Holt, Rinehart and
    Winston.

National Commission on Excellence in Education. 1983. *A Nation at Risk: The Imperative for Educational Reform.* Washington, D.C.: U.S. Government Printing Office.

Neubert, Gloria A., and Sally J. McNells. 1986. Improving Writing in the Disciplines. *Educational Leadership* 433 (April): 54–58.

16 Speechmapping: Navigating through Speech Preparation and Delivery

Marilyn Thanos and Brenda Avadian
Alverno College

What will help students better plan a tightly focused, clearly organized speech if they have difficulty seeing the relationships among their ideas? What will free students from reading their manuscripts or notes so that they can relate to their audience? Since we ask students not to read their speeches nor to recite them from memory, what will help them recall the order of their ideas? These were the questions Alverno College Communication Department faculty asked themselves as they sought a method to encourage students to focus their thoughts, to develop their main points with relevant supporting material, and to sound spontaneous and natural when delivering their speeches.

As speech instructors, we had traditionally taught outlining as a tool for effective speech preparation and delivery. In seeking answers to our questions, however, we found that outlining does not show the dynamic relationships among ideas, nor does it help students limit their focus.

In order to address these shortcomings, we designed a technique which is a visual representation showing the organization, development, and relationship of ideas (Alverno College Communication Department 1976, 1979, 1980; Alverno College Faculty 1976 [see footnote below]). We found that this method can assist students not only in the speech planning process but in the delivery process as well. We call this technique mapping because it shows how one idea leads to another idea, not unlike the road map which shows how to get from one city to the next.

Authors' Note: Alverno College Faculty began seeking ways to assist students to develop all communication abilities in 1973. By 1976, one of the techniques we had devised was a mapping technique which has been used since in all the speaking courses as well as in the teaching of analytic listening, analytic reading abilities, and writing.

Much has been written about mapping in recent years. For example, Gowin (1981) and others (Wicker 1985, Novak and Gowin 1984, Buckley and Boyle 1981) report on concept mapping—visually showing the hierarchical relationships among the concepts of a given framework. Other researchers have reported on mind mapping, which involves brainstorming to branch associated ideas around a given concept (Woods 1985, Buzan 1983, Buckley and Boyle 1981, Bihl-Hulme 1983). Much of this research addresses mapping as a tool for focusing one's thinking in relation to reading and writing.

In this article we will focus on how mapping techniques can facilitate the preparation and delivery of a speech. We will describe the elements of a speech shown on a map, the process of mapping, the use of a map during practice and delivery, and the advantages of mapping.

Elements of a Speech Shown on a Map

A map visually depicts all the parts of a speech. The *thesis statement* is the starting point of the map construction (Figure 1). *Major points* or divisions of the thesis statement become major branches off the thesis statement. *Supporting material* appears as subdivisions off each major branch. The subdivisions can branch out as well with *additional information*.

The *introduction* of the speech and the *conclusion* are also parts of the map with lines connecting them to the rest of the map.

The branching lines relate ideas to each other and to the thesis.

The Mapping Process

The mapping process follows three general stages of development: formulating a thesis statement, delineating and developing major points of the thesis, and incorporating the introduction and conclusion.

Formulating a Thesis Statement

As preparatory steps for mapping, students (1) identify a subject or topic area for their presentation, (2) complete their information gathering, and (3) analyze their audience, purpose, and speaking situation. Then we ask them to formulate a thesis statement—what is the point they want to get across? We teach that a thesis statement should be one sentence containing three elements: a topic which has

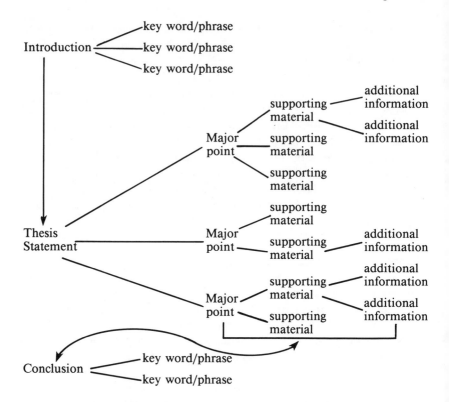

Figure 1: Generic Map

been narrowed down to represent the student's focus (limitation), a personal opinion or position regarding the topic (stance), and an indication of the organizational direction that the speech will follow (direction).

For example, we might give the following assignment in a persuasion class: "Analyze persuasive messages according to a framework you studied in this class." A student may choose to talk about Aristotle's forms of proof and how present-day persuasive messages reflect their use. The student's thesis statement might be "Present-day special-issue campaigns and advertisements effectively reflect Aristotle's forms of proof to promote ideas and products."

Reviewing the three criteria for an effective thesis, the student might limit the topic in several ways—"present-day" rather than times in the past; "special-issue campaigns and advertisements" clearly limits the samples to be analyzed. "Aristotle's forms of proof" specifies what framework the student will use. The student indicates a stance by giving a personal opinion that present-day promotions *effectively*

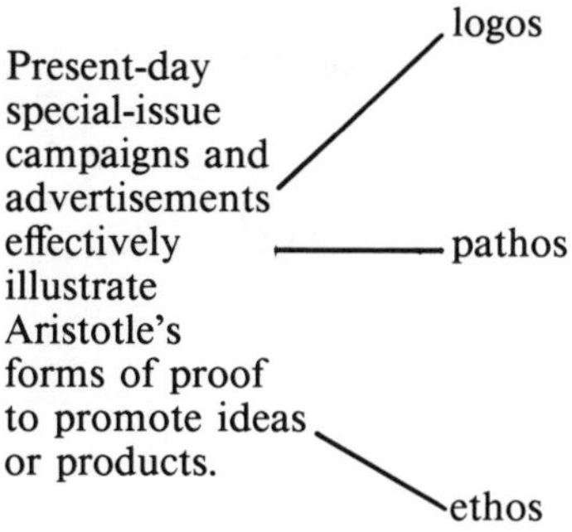

Figure 2: Thesis and Major Points

reflect Aristotle's proofs. The audience has a clear sense of the direction or organization the speech will take. They will expect the student to present and define Aristotle's forms of proof and to show examples which reflect these proofs.

We should note that although there may be other criteria by which students may formulate a thesis, the important point is that they must carefully think out their thesis statement as the basis for the mapping process. We find that time spent on this aspect is worth the effort. A well-developed thesis statement is easy to "crack open" into major divisions which become the main branches of the map.

Delineating and Developing Major Points

The next stage in the process is to branch out the major points from the thesis. The number of major points depends on the scope of the thesis statement and the speech's time limit. We recommend that students begin by writing the thesis in the middle of the left-hand side of the page in order to have room to branch out their ideas. In the previous example the student might identify Aristotle's three forms of proof as major points, making them three branches extending from the thesis statement (Figure 2). The student then develops each major point individually. Beginning with the first major point, the student would branch out each sub-point and additional supporting details as they relate to each other (Figure 3). The student then would develop a second major point in the same manner, and so on (Figure 4).

After the student has completely developed the major points with the information available, we advise him or her to look back to the thesis to see if it still encompasses the content developed in the major points and supporting material. If it does not, then the student must

Figure 3: Development of First Major Point

make revisions in either the thesis, the major points, or the supporting detail to make certain every item on the map relates to the idea to which it connects.

Incorporating Introduction and Conclusion

The final stage in the map preparation process is to incorporate an introduction and conclusion. Depending upon the students' level of confidence in speaking and familiarity with the specific topic, they may either write the introduction and conclusion out in full or map out key words or phrases. Consistent with the frequently cited functions of effective introductions and conclusions, we suggest that besides catching attention and creating interest, the introduction should provide an effective lead-in to the thesis. The conclusion should proceed from what goes before it by encapsulating the essence of the speech.

Working with the Map

After students demonstrate the basic mapping technique, they learn how to organize ideas on a map, how to practice with a map, and how to use a map for delivery.

Methods of Organizing Ideas on a Map

Once students have developed a working map by formulating a thesis and delineating major points and supporting material, they then

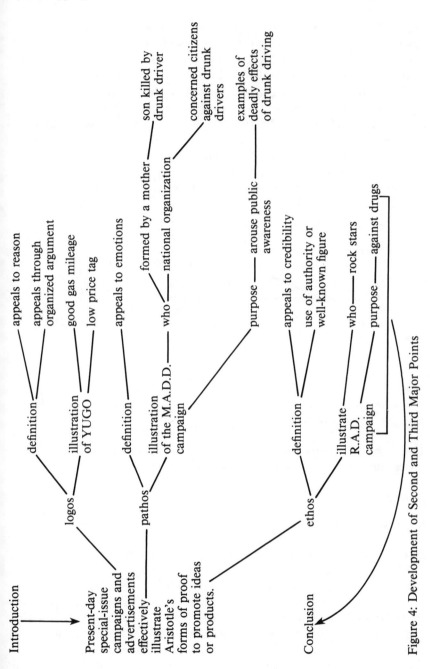

Figure 4: Development of Second and Third Major Points

decide how to arrange the information to achieve their purpose, given the topic and audience they will address. Analyzing how the audience might react to the topic and position will affect the decision as to what organizational plan to use.

If the student is giving a persuasive talk, he or she might choose from a number of organizational patterns. Suppose that the audience is hostile. To defuse their hostility, the student may choose a problem-solution pattern. If the audience is neutral, Monroe's Motivated Sequence (Ehninger et al. 1986) might provide a good pattern. A map should reflect whatever organizational pattern the student chooses. A map of the five steps of Monroe's Motivated Sequence could look like this:

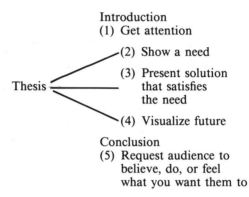

Introduction
(1) Get attention

(2) Show a need

(3) Present solution
    that satisfies
    the need

Thesis

(4) Visualize future

Conclusion
(5) Request audience to
    believe, do, or feel
    what you want them to

Figure 5: Map of Monroe's Motivated Sequence

Using the above map as a model, the student maps ideas so that they correspond to each of Monroe's steps.

Practicing with a Map

Once the student has a drawing of the speech that shows the order in which he or she wants to present ideas, practice can begin. The student has filled in the key words of the supporting material to be used to prove, explain, or clarify the major points. Carefully drawn lines show ideas relating and leading to each other. Graphically, the map also indicates proportion—which ideas have more supporting material and therefore will take more time to cover adequately when the student actually presents the talk. While practicing, students record the amount of time each major point takes to deliver. They then compare the total time of delivery to the allowed time limit. If the speech is over the time limit, they must decide whether to revise the focus of the thesis or limit the amount of supporting detail in any one of the major points. For example, if students have eight minutes to deliver four major points and the first point takes six minutes, they may consider narrowing the focus of the thesis to address only the first major point. Then, students will need to delineate major points for the revised thesis.

To practice, the students read through their entire map beginning with the introduction, which leads to the thesis and then the point-by-point development. They read one major point and its supporting material, as well as any sub-points and further evidence. The next major point is covered in the same manner, and so on, ending with the conclusion (see Figure 4). The object is to learn the order of the ideas. Then students practice by speaking aloud, looking at the map when needed to see what comes next. The map allows the student to see the entire speech at a glance—no problem with note-card shuffling or trying to find one's place in a hurry. If the speech needs further revision, it is easy to change the respective part of the map by adding or deleting information yet preserving the overall organization. In addition, the student may include delivery prompts throughout the map wherever they are necessary. Practice is essential until the student can speak fluently about each major point.

Using the Map for Delivery

The map becomes the set of "speaking notes" to which a speaker can refer while actually presenting a talk. At any time the speaker can see the entire speech at a glance, can tell what has already been covered, and can see what ideas come next. Since the map contains only key words or phrases, students must speak the speech rather than read or recite from memory a written word-for-word manuscript. As a result, students are apt to sound more spontaneous, conversational, and natural. This enables them to have better eye contact with the audience and to exhibit more vocal variety than if they read. As a result, each student tends to feel more effective and successful as a speaker.

Mapping or Outlining?

Traditionally, speech instructors have taught outlining as part of speech preparation and have encouraged students to use an outline during the delivery of a speech. We have found, however, that a map overcomes some of the shortcomings of an outline. Outlines by their very nature are linear in form. Thus they do not show the relationship among ideas in a holistic manner. Mapping, on the other hand, is multidirectional. A map holistically shows precise relationships. Furthermore, mapping allows the designer to review quickly idea development and proportion (Loacker et al. 1984).

A student who uses a mapping process in the preparatory stages of a speech can literally see the speech take form. This makes it easier for the student to keep the speech tightly focused and to provide adequate development. It also makes it easier for us to assist a student who has difficulty in seeing how ideas relate. We can point out on the map where ideas do not "fit" or relate and how they might be extraneous to the speech's focus/thesis.

As noted earlier, the use of a map promotes a more conversational delivery style. A map can also help students feel more confident when speaking. Students worry less about a lost thought because the map provides a ready view of the entire speech. If students have the tendency to ramble, they will find that by following the map they will stay on track and will more tightly focus their ideas, clearly relating them to the thesis and to each other.

Most of our students learn the mapping process quickly. Many have provided testimonials regarding the efficiency and effectiveness of mapping as a speech preparation and delivery tool.

We encourage speech instructors to teach the mapping process. Our ultimate goal is to assist students to become effective oral communicators. We find that mapping is a tool which helps us to achieve our goal by assisting students to plot their ideas in a focused way and to navigate themselves and their audiences through the pathways of their thoughts.

Bibliography

Alverno College Communication Department. 1976. *Modules for Speaking and Writing*. Milwaukee, Wis.: Alverno College.

————. 1979. Making a Map for Speaking. (Videotape in *Speaking Modules* series.) Milwaukee, Wis.: Alverno College.

————. 1980. Speaking from a Map. (Videotape in *Speaking Modules* series.) Milwaukee, Wis.: Alverno College.

Bihl-Hulme, J. 1985. Creative Thinking in Problem-Based Learning. In *Problem-Based Learning in Education for the Professions*, edited by D. Boud. Sydney: HERDSA.

Buckley, M., and O. Boyle. 1981. *Mapping the Writing Journey*. Berkeley, Calif.: Bay Area Writing Project, School of Education, University of California.

Buzan, T. 1983. *Use Both Sides of Your Brain.* New York: E. P. Dutton.

Ehninger, D., B. E. Gronbeck, R. E. McKerrow, and A. H. Monroe. 1986. *Principles and Types of Speech Communication.* 10th ed. Glenview, Ill.: Scott, Foresman.

Gowin, D. B. 1981. *Educating.* London: Cornell University Press.

Loacker, G., L. Cromwell, J. Fey, and D. Rutherford. 1984. *Analysis and Communications at Alverno: An Approach to Critical Thinking.* Milwaukee, Wis.: Alverno Productions.

Novak, J. D., and B. D. Gowin. 1984. *Learning How to Learn.* Cambridge, England: Cambridge University Press.

Wicker, A. W. 1985. Getting Out of Our Conceptual Ruts: Strategies for Expanding Conceptual Frameworks. *American Psychologist* 40 (10): 1094–1102.

Woods, D. 1985. Problem-Based Learning and Problem Solving. In *Problem-Based Learning in Education for the Professions,* edited by D. Boud. Sydney: HERDSA.

17 The Classroom Debate: A Stimulus for Listening, Speaking, and Arguing

Carol Hovanec
Ramapo College

A formal debate can serve as an excellent technique to teach argument. Coming early in the prewriting process, this activity can focus speaking and listening skills to help students become interested in a topic, see both sides of an issue, and develop adequate support for a position.

I use debating in a freshman composition class at a four-year liberal arts college in a unit on argument which comes about mid-semester. The unit has the following components:

1. Introduction to the topic

2. Class debate

3. Group workshop to sort out issues

4. Group workshop to formulate individual positions

5. Group workshop to present first draft

6. The finished paper

Each of the five preliminary steps requires at least one period, but the steps may need to be alternated with other classes to allow students time to prepare the assigned work. These interrupting lessons should be kept to a minimum, however.

Any current topic is suitable for this unit and can be chosen by the instructor or the class. I have found that there is little advantage in letting students elect their own subject; since at this stage of their education they have limited knowledge of current events, the process of choosing can take an unnecessarily long time, and some issues may be too idiosyncratic or localized (e.g., a campus or town policy) to generate adequate material for support.

Articles for background reading can be found in freshman readers, if a text is being used which has sufficient material on the topic (this past semester our classes were using Miller's *The Informed Argument*, which included a number of selections on controversial subjects). But

I have also supplied material myself, or had students research the topic independently. In the latter case, this exercise can provide an excellent introduction to research skills by enabling students to find their articles during a supervised library workshop and document final papers according to MLA guidelines.

This past semester I used animal experimentation for this unit, introducing the class to the subject by asking them to read an essay from *The American Psychologist* by C. R. Gallistel (reprinted in Miller's *The Informed Argument*) and write answers to several questions about content and strategy. I began the class by handing out copies of an article in a local newspaper reporting on a recent protest by animal rights activists as well as a letter to an editor of the same periodical by the president of the Humane Society of the United States. These two items, together with Dr. Gallistel's article, presented the two sides of the issue and underlined its immediacy. After discussing the subject for almost the entire period, we formulated a proposition together, reviewed the directions for the debate, and chose positions.

The written assignment for the debate (see page 102) establishes roles for every class member, including the instructor. There is a chair, associate chair, panelists, and audience members. The chair summarizes the subject, introduces the panel, and keeps order; the associate chair handles the question-and-answer period. These students are instructed to time presentations, rebuttal, and all responses carefully. Panelists, of course, present position papers and answer questions. Audience members bring their own questions to ensure participation. I sit in the audience and join in the questioning, leaving the management to the chair and associate chair, who know they are graded on how well they maintain control and include the audience in the discussion. Everyone is required to read at least one article by an authority on the subject. To increase interest, panelists are asked to impersonate experts and use assumed names. Before the debate begins, I remind the class to take notes (in journals, if these are required, or notebooks) to use for the upcoming workshops and composition assignment. Once the debate begins, students listen attentively during the presentations, but are lively and even vociferous in the following question-and-answer period.

Follow-up classes build on the debate to help students prepare a well-argued and organized response. In the first workshop (see directions for workshop on argument, p. 103), students are asked to discuss the issues and plan outlines for two opposing sides of the topic. At the beginning of this session, I briefly explain the terminology used in the directions (*crucial, secondary, admitted issues*), as well as provide an example from a sample argument on DDT which I will use throughout these exercises. I also urge students to gather as much information as they can to use in their final papers by finding articles other class members have read which they might also want to consult. I allow them to change groups periodically so they can receive this additional input. I also move from group to group to answer questions.

After a general discussion of the workshop outlines, I ask individuals to prepare their own versions at home, indicating their positions and support, for the following class meeting (see Writing Assignment IV: Part I, p. 103). Notice that I ask for documentation of readings at this point so they will keep track of the bibliographical information and practice its formatting. In the class meeting, I again ask them to share their outlines with a group to test the formulation of the thesis and the logic of their support. For this exercise, formal workshop directions don't seem necessary, but I again sit with groups to be sure they are analyzing the outlines constructively. I also allow time at the end of the period for sharing some of the outlines with the rest of the class as well as to explain the format for the introduction and conclusion which I want them to use for their first draft (Writing Assignment IV: Part II, p. 104). If I feel students do not have time to prepare this draft for the next class, I schedule an intervening lesson on grammar or mechanics to allow more time for this stage of the process.

The next workshop session entails preliminary evaluation of complete drafts for the paper (see Writing Assignment IV: Evaluation of Argumentative Drafts, p. 104). Notice that I include questions on placement of the thesis as well as on style. As with the other workshops, I participate in the groups, making candid suggestions but trying not to dominate the discussion. As a peer critiquing activity, this workshop helps the individual writer by forcing him or her to break the close psychological bond with the written page which often makes it difficult to see errors or hear repetitions or awkwardness. An additional benefit is that the audience knows the subject as well as the author and can make more meaningful comments on the validity of supporting points.

When the final papers were turned in this past semester, I was delighted with the quality, particularly remembering that the students were first-semester freshmen. For example, one eighteen-year-old wrote this introduction:

Although many people enjoy different animals in nature and as pets, there are other uses for these animals in scientific laboratories. It is through animal experimentation that vast improvements can be made in both the medical care and research of human beings. Scientists certainly do not enjoy inflicting pain; however, if causing an animal to suffer might benefit the human race, it is necessary and with just cause.

And a foreign student wrote this one:

Animal experimentation has been an accepted method of learning about the physiology of humans and other species for at least two hundred years. The rights and wrongs of these experiments have been debated for just as long, and the subject remains a topical one. In this day and age, when racial discrimination, feminism and homosexuals' rights are discussed, it is only natural that the rights of animals should be considered too. Animals are living beings, and many of them are capable of suffering and enjoyment to the same degree as many humans. The use of animals in research has been beneficial to science, but it is time to reevaluate the necessity and moral implications of using live animals for this purpose.

The quality of the writing, and the thinking, exceeded anything I had received when I taught argument in a vacuum without the stimulus of the debate and the follow-up process workshops. Students' skills in reading and writing had been enhanced by exposure to selections by experts who used sophisticated vocabulary and syntax. They acquired tactics for arguing, supporting, and documenting a position through the series of guided workshops. The papers which they produced could not be plagiarized (knowingly or unknowingly), because of the stages they had been required to go through. But in addition to the improvement in composition, there were other rewards. Students learned to speak in formal and informal situations and listen carefully to the presentations of their peers. In addition, those placed in positions of authority as chairs, associate chairs, and group leaders often reveled in their newfound attention and responsibility. Even poor or mediocre students realized they had something to offer to the class, and this recognition inspired them to take a new interest in all of the subsequent activities.

As director of freshman English I have shared this idea with my colleagues, and the class debate has become a popular staple of all of our writing classes at Ramapo College.

Reference

Miller, Robert K. 1986. *The Informed Argument: A Multidisciplinary Reader and Guide.* San Diego: Harcourt Brace Jovanovich.

Assignment for the Class Debate

<u>Directions:</u> Next week, we will have a class debate on an argumentative issue. Everyone will take part in this debate. It counts as Writing Assignment III, and will be preparation for Writing Assignment IV. A panel discussion can be lively and interesting. Here are the positions:

a) Chair (moderator): This person keeps order. He/she introduces the "experts" and keeps panel members from talking too long or getting off the subject.
b) Associate Chair: The associate chair handles the question-and-answer session. In case the chair is absent, the associate chair is expected to handle his/her responsibilities.
c) Panel Member: An expert on the subject, who presents a brief statement of his/her position, debates with other panel members, answers questions, etc.
d) Alternate: Stands in for panel members in their absence.
e) Member of the Audience: A concerned citizen who has come prepared with questions for the panel.

You are required to choose one of the above for the debate, remembering that you must read at least one article on the topic. The chairs and panel members will receive extra credit, and articulate members of the audience will receive a better grade.

The chair should open the panel with a brief statement as to why the subject is topical, and introduce the speakers. He/she must be constantly aware of how the debate is going and keep it balanced by cutting off irrelevant or long-winded speakers. This is a position for a not-too-shy leader. The panel member must pretend to be an expert, present a brief statement of the position of the person being impersonated, and be prepared to answer questions.

PROPOSITION:_____

CHAIR:_____

ASSOCIATE CHAIR:_____

PANELIST ONE (PRO): DR._____

PANELIST TWO (PRO): DR._____

PANELIST THREE (CON): DR._____

PANELIST FOUR (CON): DR._____

ALTERNATES (1 PRO and 1 CON):_____

Workshop on Argument

Directions: In your group, discuss the following questions and formulate answers. Everyone should fill out one of the sheets, but choose a spokesperson to present the group's answers in the following general discussion.

1. Construct a rough outline for both the "pro" and "con" sides of the proposition for the debate. In other words, what were the crucial issues and any secondary issues which emerged?
2. Determine 2–3 points which could be used to support both crucial issues (for example, if you were arguing on the use of DDT, a "pro" point would be that it's inexpensive, but a "con" would be that it is dangerous).
3. Once you have these 2–3 general points (which we call primary support), decide how you would go about proving them. Here, use articles in your text, find statistics, quotes from authorities, etc. Note the author, article title, and page numbers. You may use support from other sources as long as you can prove it.
4. Looking at your outline, decide if either side has a point which the opposition might refute or argue against in any way—or would they all have to be dealt with as admitted issues?

Writing Assignment IV: Part I

Directions: For next class, prepare an outline for a paper on animal rights. Your first sentence should be a thesis sentence which presents your position clearly. Your next sentence should present primary support. Then you should indicate what secondary support you are going to use to back up your points. Then, show how you will refute points your opponent might raise. Notice the following example:

I. DDT has more disadvantages than advantages. In particular, this insecticide is dangerous and outmoded.

dangerous> does not break down in the environment (Dr. Thomas Adams, "DDT: A New Look," *Science* [Oct. 9, 1986], p. 88).*

outmoded> new discoveries make it unnecessary (Dr. Anthony Brown, *Modern Biology* [New York: Bantam, 1986], pp. 88–89).*

II. DDT is inexpensive and effective.

inexpensive> yes, but money not as important as potential damage to future organisms.

effective> yes, but there are other alternatives, such as pyrethrin compounds.

(In neither case are you truly admitting, since you are able to argue against the points effectively.)

The paper will be used in class for a group workshop. Also, I will show you how to add an introduction and conclusion. Part II of this assignment will necessitate writing a complete draft for the following class.

* References are examples only and not actual articles.

Writing Assignment IV: Part II

Directions: Write a draft of a complete paper for our next class. You should
have an introduction, a middle (one long paragraph or several smaller
paragraphs), and a conclusion. You should have primary and secondary
support, the latter documented with the name of the author and the page
numbers from the source. Your paper need not be typed, but it should be
as neat as you can make it. You will be asked to read it to a group to receive
feedback, so remember that you will have an audience, not necessarily the
same one you had today. If you spend time on this segment and do it
carefully, you will not have a lot to do for the final version of this paper.
This is an important stage.

Writing Assignment IV: Evaluation of Argumentative Drafts

Directions: As each group member reads his/her paper, listen carefully and
answer the following questions.

1. Is the first sentence of the introduction a lead-in sentence and not the
   thesis?
2. Does the thesis sentence occur three times, rephrased, and in the proper
   positions in the paragraphs?
3. Does the author provide adequate support for the position he/she favors?
4. Are the opponent's points referred to as well?
5. Does the paper seem to have good flow, no awkwardness?
6. Is there excessive repetition?

18 Student Panel Presentations: A Collaborative Oral Exercise

Bruce R. Henderson
Fairleigh Dickinson University

I would like to describe an assignment which I used successfully in a freshman composition course and which included an oral presentation by each student, building their confidence and encouraging them to process and evaluate information orally. Further, the assignment is widely adaptable to other courses and subject matter.

This assignment found its way into my composition class because it seemed important to include some oral component in the teaching of writing. Our language is, after all, derived from an oral tradition. True appreciation of the power, nuance, and beauty of language cannot ignore the oral arts. Also, presenting an argument or opinion aloud to others reinforces some cardinal principles we encourage on the written page: clarity, logic, and awareness of and communication with the audience. Finally, as teachers who are called upon as a matter of course to make oral presentations both in class and in meetings and other professional functions, we are all used to standing before an audience and expressing ourselves. But canvas a typical class of freshmen and you may find, as I have, that very few felt confident in doing so, and some had in fact consciously avoided any such experience.

So, with basic rationale and reasons out in the open, here is the assignment I used to try to give students a worthwhile oral forum. This assignment is applicable to almost any course which attempts to cover a particular content area. In this course, most of the readings and subsequent discussion centered around nuclear issues. The main text used was *The Nuclear Predicament* (Gregory 1986). Students were divided into small groups of three or four (panels, if you like), and each group was asked to come up with a particular aspect of the nuclear predicament that members would like to explore further. Since this was the concluding assignment of the semester, students had by that time developed sufficient familiarity and expertise in the content area to make a reasonable and workable choice.

After each group had settled on a topic, I asked them to subdivide the research and presentation. That is, the group would function as a panel which would present the chosen topic by means of individual oral reports and would also be prepared to field questions on either these individual areas of expertise or on the entire topic. In this way each student became responsible for not only his or her piece of the presentation but for familiarity with the overall topic as well. One result of this arrangement was that pressure to complete the research and present a coherent report transferred to the students themselves rather than being exerted by the instructor, since it was in their own interests, both from the standpoint of evaluation and to avoid embarrassment in front of their peers, to do a decent job. Notice that this peer pressure is a direct result of being put "on the spot" by facing an oral and public presentation. How many students have, at one time or another, settled for handing in last-minute, shoddy work, knowing that at worst the bad grade or harsh evaluation could be absorbed in the privacy and anonymity of the quietly returned and folded paper?

The entire assignment was scheduled over a period of about two weeks, to allow for the various individual and collaborative stages. One panel chose as their topic the "Star Wars" defense system. Among the four members, one chose the subtopic of current research and technology. Another would present arguments in favor of the system, based upon opinions of prominent scientists and government leaders but also including her own summary view; the third student would likewise handle arguments against the system. The fourth student would address the question of Soviet response: Soviet research as known, their public statements regarding Star Wars, and their projected policies in response to Star Wars. Obviously these subtopics overlapped in many ways; each student would be obliged, for example, to understand the basic technologies of the system, i.e., how it is supposed to work and how likely it would be to work in the near future.

Other general or panel topics included nuclear winter, a study of current international arsenals, emergency readiness procedures on the college campus, projected attack scenarios, and a history of the development of nuclear weapons. The next stage of the assignment after choosing and subdividing the general topics was individual research. In some cases this could still be accomplished collaboratively, and certainly students were able to share some resources. If instructors using this assignment wished to reinforce individual research and writing effort, they could simply require each student to submit a written version, complete with documentation, of his or her individual area of inquiry.

During the two weeks the assignment was in progress I allowed some class time for groups to meet and confer on their research and presentation strategies, both with me and among themselves. But most of the work was accomplished outside of class and in addition to their ongoing essay assignments, readings, and other usual course activities.

When presentation day arrived, students essentially conducted the classroom activities. It is particularly rewarding for an instructor to be able to sit back and for once *not* feel responsible for conducting the proceedings or for even saying much. The panel presentations ran themselves, yet each student in the class was involved at all times, either as a presenter, as a panel member, or as a respondent. The student orally presenting the fruits of his or her research gained experience in communicating complex information and personal opinion to an audience of informed peers, whereas panel members listened to double-check information and prepare themselves for questions. The audience of students listened out of interest in a shared overall area of inquiry (nuclear issues), to gain background for questions to presenters and other panel members, and to compare their own presentations to those for which they served as audience. Since each student would take his or her turn in front of the entire class, politeness and etiquette were givens: all realized that at some point the situation would be reversed; therefore, they extended the courtesy and attention that each presenter deserved. Though some were initially nervous, students enjoyed their presentations, followed them with lively and informed discussion and debate, and welcomed the change in routine and the opportunity to take charge of class proceedings.

One value of this assignment lies in reinforcing the principles of good essay writing in a form other than the usual student-composed, teacher-evaluated paper. With oral presentations, work is shared and critiqued by the entire class; a definite audience has to be addressed (other than the usual implied and predictable final audience for papers—the instructor); students have the opportunity to work collaboratively (which, beyond possible small-group critiquing, is difficult to arrange in a composition class); and, finally, students depend upon each other for and come to value thoroughness of research and clarity of presentation.

The general structure of this assignment is adaptable to many other content areas; indeed it is difficult to imagine a college course in which such a procedure could not be used. It seems particularly adaptable to the literature course, especially one in which some of the readings are complex enough to merit research and analysis by several students working on different aspects of a selection, or one in which several reading selections might be profitably compared and contrasted by a panel.

For appreciation of the spoken word, a variation which I have found useful is to have individual students read aloud to the class some piece of writing by which they are impressed, in whatever form it may be (poem, editorial, novel excerpt, and so forth) and then explain why they think it is a worthwhile or well-done piece of writing and, finally, entertain any questions from the class/audience about either the writing itself or the author. Again, such an assignment can include a written version of the presentation as well, and would also be particularly adaptable to a literature course. Notice, too, that both the panel and individual versions of this assignment offer ample opportunities for instructors to grade or otherwise evaluate students from the standpoints of individual presentations, research, written versions, panel participation, and/or audience response.

This assignment affords students an opportunity to apply principles of research, composition, and presentation in an alternative approach which has the added value of promoting speaking and listening abilities. Much of the preparatory work can be accomplished outside of class. It is adaptable to most grade levels and subject areas. It reinforces students' responsibilities *to each other* as a community of learners by involving them in a collaborative and self-directed activity. Finally, it gives students valuable experience in addressing and directing a group, which builds confidence and provides realistic preparation for later life both in and beyond the college years.

Reference

Gregory, Donna. 1986. *The Nuclear Predicament.* New York: St. Martin's Press.

19 A Global Introduction to International Business Communications

Ray Wallace
University of Tennessee, Knoxville

About every six months one national periodical or another publishes a feature on the lack of geographic knowledge among Americans, especially among high school and college students. The examples have become well-known: California students who think Toronto is in Italy, students from Miami who cannot place their home city on a map of Florida, Midwest students who have no idea where Russia is, and students from some southern states who are unsure where Mexico lies. While the statistics and examples (these features usually carry "amusing" maps of the geographically distorted world our students see) may be very interesting to the general readership of these periodicals, to educators they are reminders of another area we must focus on in our already overcrowded syllabi.

So, as more educators begin to design assignments that will reinforce knowledge about the world these students live in, perhaps these same educators will one day enter a classroom to be faced by the knowledgeable students they desire: students who can recognize the continents, know north from south, east from west, and have at least a working knowledge of the major political, economic, and social forces designing the world they live in.

Each semester a group of twenty international business majors, usually evenly divided between American and ESL students, enroll in my International Business Communications course. My main goal is to help these students improve their business communications skills by focusing on the four linguistic skills: speaking, listening, reading, and writing. I have designed an introductory assignment to this course that focuses on these skills and, at the same time, reinforces the importance of geographic knowledge for success in international business communications. The assignment usually takes three phases to complete.

Phase One

On the first day the course meets, I enter with two detailed maps: one of the world and one of the United States. Students immediately become fearful, since they suspect they will be "tested" on that which they know very little about. Therefore, I tell them to relax, inform them of the course requirements and prerequisites, and mention the importance of acquiring a greater knowledge of the world to succeed in international business. My discussion leads to the inevitable fact that, since they are all going into careers in international business, soon they will have to deal with a person from a country other than their own.

I ask the students to discuss what questions an interviewer might ask a foreign subject to discover enough pertinent information about that person's culture and country to help in trading with his or her part of the world. The questions the students develop are written on the board:

1. What is your name?
2. Where were you born?
3. Can you tell a little about your family life?
4. Can you describe the economy of your country?
5. Can you describe your education system?
6. What is the climate like in your country?
7. What type of political system exists in your country?
8. Is international business important in your country?
9. What countries have you visited?
10. Who do you consider the most famous living person from your country?

I ask the students to pair themselves, one American student to one ESL student (if there are more Americans than ESL students, then a 2:1 ratio is fine). The two students are given about twenty minutes to interview each other to find the answers to these and any other questions they feel are important to the process of finding out about each other's culture and country. They are allowed to take all the notes they wish on the answers to these questions. I usually ask the American students to answer the questions in the first ten-minute period because they seem less culturally worried about divulging such information to a stranger. Therefore, by the time the ESL students, who may be a little more reticent about disclosing such information to a foreigner, have heard their American counterparts talk about themselves and their backgrounds, most of them answer the questions freely. Finally, students show their partners where exactly they are from on either of the maps provided.

In this initial phase, students make conscious efforts to overcome breakdowns in auditory communication. They listen intently; they ask for clarification, for repetition, and for more details. Students often share their notes to see if everything they have noted is accurate.

Phase Two

In order to give students their first opportunity to speak in front of an audience, I ask each student to come to the front of the class to discuss what they have learned from talking to their new colleague. Each student has to focus on the geographic, economic, and social knowledge gained from talking to this person. I ask each speaker to point to the area on the map that the presentation deals with, and I ask the audience (other members of the class) to ask questions based on the information presented by the speaker. At first the audience is too intimidated to ask questions, but after I ask the first few they usually begin to ask quite interesting and detailed questions.

Obviously, many of these presenters are not able to answer some of the more complex questions based on their limited knowledge of the area in question. I then call on anyone in the class to answer the question; any question left unanswered is used later in a research scavenger hunt in the library. After all the students have presented their information, I allow them to mix again for five minutes. This time they are allowed to mingle and talk with different students, and all seem genuinely interested in their peers, both ESL and American.

Phase Three

As a way of checking students' listening and writing proficiency, I ask each student to write a one-page summary of one person in the class other than the person he or she initially interviewed and subsequently presented information about to the rest of the class. Again, I want the students to pick someone from a country other than their own. In this one-page description, they are to write as informatively as possible, giving all the key information they can remember from the initial presentation.

This assignment, which covers approximately the first week of the course, is in no way meant to be a panacea for all of the students' communication problems. Similarly, this assignment will not teach students all they will ever need to know about world geography, nor all about the social and economic factors playing on the world. However, it will spark interest and curiosity in the world around them.

Such an assignment emphasizes two important points early in the semester. The first point of emphasis is that students will be expected to use all the communication skills they are being taught each day; they will have to actively listen, speak, read, and write. Secondly, this introductory assignment emphasizes that in order to succeed in international business, students have to overcome a very egocentric view of the world. While ESL students seem to suffer less from geographic unawareness, both groups of students need to become more knowledgeable about the United States and the world with which the U.S. trades. Such acquisition of knowledge cannot be achieved by passively memorizing statistics about various countries. Instead, this assignment points to the need for active participation in the learning process, a process which can only occur through listening, speaking, reading, and writing about various areas in the world.

This introductory exercise leads to many more geographically enhanced communication-based exercises designed to help students grow into well-educated business executives. In trying to help our students understand the part they can play in their world, one of the key goals of any liberal education, teachers must show them the importance each state and country plays in the overall economic, political, and social global framework.

20 Structuring Speaking and Listening in the Classroom

Nancy Wyatt
The Pennsylvania State University
Delaware County Campus

One of the reasons students find it difficult to talk freely in the classroom is that they don't know how to organize their thoughts. The most common goal listed by the students in my public speaking course is "to speak clearly." "Speaking clearly" most often translates into "to organize my thoughts clearly to express what I mean." Students report that they feel uncomfortable in discussions because they are afraid (or they know from experience) that others will misinterpret what they are saying or that they will get lost in their own argument and lose their train of thought. The result is that students avoid taking part in discussions, and they avoid classes where they will be expected to make speeches or presentations.

Another problem that students have in the classroom is keeping track of lectures and discussions. Students report that they can't write down everything, and they often can't tell what's important from what's not important. The consequence is that they often try to write down the "facts," but they miss the generalizations that would give meaning to those facts. Their lecture notes are often unorganized and inaccurate. They have trouble following directions.

The solution to both of these problems is to teach students how to organize their ideas when they talk and how to listen for organizational patterns when they listen. One simple system for organizing ideas is called "structuring" (Zolten and Phillips 1985). The idea behind this system is that we have several ways of organizing ideas that are natural to us in our daily lives. By identifying and using these natural patterns of organizing ideas, we can present our ideas clearly in speeches and in discussion. By listening for the basic organizational patterns (structures), we can identify main points and distinguish important information from unimportant information. In

113

this article, I will describe five basic structural patterns and explain how to teach structuring.

Basic Structural Patterns

Time structure is a narrative or storytelling structure. We use time structure when we explain how things got this way or explain how to do something. For example, "The Battle of Gettysburg took place over three days" and "There are five steps to preparing a book report" are time-structured messages. Once you know that the message is time-structured, it's easy to pick out the main points. The main points are each of the elements of the story, which *must* follow one another in sequence. Speakers can cue listeners to the use of a time structure by listing the main points before they begin speaking: "Making a speech requires six steps: (1) analyzing the audience and the situation, (2) choosing a structure, (3) adding details, (4) practicing, (5) delivering the speech, and (6) evaluating the response." Listeners who hear such a statement of the structure can easily pick out the main points; the speaker has just listed them.

Space structure tells about how something is made or put together. When we use a space structure we are talking about all the parts of something. For example, "The motorcycle engine has seven main working parts" and "The American government is made up of three main branches" are space-structured messages. Again, it's up to the speaker to make the main points clear at the beginning of the speech. Hearing the main points will tell the listeners what the structure is and will let them make categories in their notes for those main points.

Classification is another common way of organizing our thoughts, but it's probably the trickiest to use. I call this the "three kinds of" or the "three ways to" speech. We often divide things into types or kinds: "There are three kinds of schools: private, parochial, and public." The problem is that there are lots of different ways to divide things up. For instance, we could also say, "There are three kinds of schools: elementary school, secondary school, and college." In the first case, we are talking about how schools are financed, while in the second we are talking about the various levels of instruction. *It's important not to mix up the classification schemes* when you're using this structure. When listeners hear "seven kinds of stars" or "two ways to check for fleas," they will know there is a classification system to the message, and they will also know how many main points to look for. It's up to the speaker to tell the listeners how many classifications there are and what the system is that connects these classifications.

Comparison is another common way of thinking about the world. Speakers can talk about how things are alike or how they are different: "Cross-country and downhill skiing offer exercise and fun for everyone," or "Cross-country and downhill skiing require different kinds of equipment." Speakers can often explain difficult ideas by comparing them to something the listeners already know about: "Football and rugby are both types of contact sports." Whenever we evaluate anything, we are using a comparison structure: "The Subaru is a good family car, because it has lots of space, is economical to run, and is dependable." Listeners should be able to pick out the three main ideas in this structure—space, economy, and dependability—as the criteria and then expect to hear how the Subaru performs on each of these standards. Speakers should know that they must provide information about each of these points if they want to be persuasive.

Cause/effect structure represents another common way of thinking about the world that answers the questions "how" and "why." Typical ideas represented in this structure are "Smoking and drinking are major causes of heart disease" and "If we add water to lithium, we will get an explosive reaction." Listeners who hear these kinds of statements can set up categories of things to listen for. The main points of the first message are (1) smoking, (2) drinking, and (3) heart disease. Speakers using this structure have to be careful not to add things that don't relate to the main ideas. For example, smoking is also linked to lung cancer, but that's not part of this particular message. By clearly specifying the main ideas in one sentence, speakers can decide what to put in the message and what to leave out.

How to Teach Structuring

The above system of organizing is probably familiar to most teachers of writing and speaking. The important thing is to get students to practice using the system both when they are speaking and when they are listening. There are a number of ways of doing this.

One of the most effective ways of practicing this system in the classroom is to assign students to give short speeches using each of the various forms of structure. I usually ask students to pick a topic and prepare five speeches on the same topic using each of the five structures. In this way they can use the same basic information and concentrate on the organizational pattern instead of trying to figure out "what to say" for five different speeches. I ask the students who are listening to write down the structure they think the speaker is using and what they think the main points are. Often the listeners disagree about the structure and the main points, and then it is possible to discuss how the speakers can make their structures clearer.

It is also possible to use impromptu speeches to reinforce this way of organizing. Give the students a general topic and ask them to prepare a short message on that topic. Easy topics include "What I wish someone had told me before I started (high school) (college)" and "The main problem facing my (school) (community) today is . . ." Again, ask the listeners to identify the structure and main points of the speeches. Discussing these speeches in class serves to (1) reinforce the importance of organizing your thoughts, (2) teach the method, and (3) teach the students how to critique messages. It also serves to accustom the students to receiving constructive criticism.

Another way to teach this method is to find a message that has no main structure (I use a typical student speech) and ask the students to identify the structure(s) in the message. After they have identified several structures, ask the students what they think the speaker's main purpose was. When they agree on a purpose, ask them to identify a structure that would make the message clearer. Then they can reconstruct the speech, identifying and supporting the main points with information from the speech. They may discover that the speaker confused the issue by putting in unnecessary information. Or they may discover that the speaker is lacking vital information and should do more research. These are both important points to consider when creating a message.

Writing teachers can use the same exercises, substituting an essay for a speech and discussing the organizational patterns in class. I have taught this system for many years, both to beginning students and to adults in my college classes. The system is really simple enough to be grasped by high school students, but the adults almost always comment on how useful they found structuring in creating speeches and in their work.

Reference

Zolten, Jerome J., and Gerald M. Phillips. 1985. *Speaking to an Audience.* Indianapolis: Bobbs-Merrill.

21 Weaving In Listening and Speaking throughout the School Day

Lynn Plourde
Anson, Maine

Teachers believe in the value of oral language skills. They want to fit listening and speaking into their schedule, but there's no time. The solution: weave these skills in throughout the day. Rather than taking a set block of time each day to develop students' listening and speaking skills, teach listening and speaking throughout the day.

First of all, there are things you as a teacher already do each day that can be adapted to develop students' listening and speaking skills, such as giving directions.

Give Directions Only Once

Most classroom teachers I've observed give directions at least three times or more until all students understand what's expected. By repeating directions, you're sending students the message that it's all right not to listen the first time. Why should they?

Start a new habit today: only say directions *one* time. I think this new habit is so important that I'm tempted to repeat it, but I won't for fear of sounding like a hypocrite.

Giving directions only once will be hard at first, but with practice you'll master this new habit. The result will be students who are better listeners. They'll have to be—you'll be forcing them to do so.

As you add this new habit to your classroom repertoire, I also suggest that you allow students to ask specific questions about directions that they did not understand. Students should be able to ask you or other students about misunderstood directions. You may wonder, "Then why not just repeat the directions?" There's a big difference. By automatically repeating directions, you're assuming students didn't understand them. You're letting students be passive listeners, and you're the one who's deciding what they did or did not "get." But by having students question directions they did not understand, you are forcing them to become active listeners. For example, a student who asks, "What did you tell us to do in the experiment after we stirred our liquid?" demonstrates that he or she listened and comprehended part of the directions and is letting you know exactly what part needs to be clarified. That's much more active listening than simply asking, "What'd you say?" or "Huh?"

Throw Students Vocabulary Curves

Another way you can improve your students' oral language skills is by throwing them vocabulary curves throughout the day. For example, rather than simply saying, "Everyone line up for recess," say, "Everyone who's a biped line up" or "Everyone line up to the left of the thermostat." By giving students directions with unusual words, you'll force them to listen to you. They'll have to question you about the meaning of unknown words—otherwise they won't be able to follow the directions. Also by using new vocabulary words several times over the course of a few weeks, students will actually begin to understand the more difficult ones.

Here are some ways you can incorporate new vocabulary words throughout the day:

- when students line up (e.g., "Everyone with spectacles line up first. Everyone born during a spring month line up second.")

- when passing out or collecting papers (e.g., "I will pass a paper to everyone who has their phalanges on their desk," "I will collect all the math papers that are lying diagonally on your desks.")

- when getting students to move from one section of the room to another (e.g., "After you point to something brittle in the room, then go stand by the piano" or "When I name something edible, then go sit in the reading corner. Hat, watch, blue, Tuesday, pickle . . .")

- when grouping students (e.g., "Everyone wearing denim will be on one team. Everyone wearing corduroy will be on another team.")

- when students trade papers (e.g., "Everyone give your paper to the student who is sitting diagonally forward to the right of you" or "Everyone give your paper to the student who is sitting two places counterclockwise from you.")

Require Students to Ask for What They Want

Another way to develop students' listening and speaking skills, especially for primary children, is to require them to tell you exactly what they want. I've been in many classrooms where a child shoves his or her chest toward the teacher and the teacher automatically zips up the child's jacket. Or the child holds out some money and the teacher says, "Oh, so you want lunch for the whole week." In these cases the teacher does the talking, not the child. Instead, you should play dumb. Don't zip the child's jacket or take the child's lunch money until they tell you exactly what they want. Otherwise, why should children talk in these situations when gestures work just as well?

Require Students to Answer in Complete Sentences

Encourage your students to answer questions using complete sentences. If they can get away with one-word answers, they will. But if there is the expectation that they must answer in complete sentences, they will do so. I have heard many children progress from a one-word answer when asked, "Why are the sky and ocean alike?" ("Blue.") to a complete response ("The sky and ocean are alike because they are both blue."). Children even begin to prompt each other to "Say the *whole* thing." They develop a habit of speaking in complete sentences—and that's not a bad habit to have.

Increase Students' Responsibilities

Consider the fact that every classroom has visitors during the school year. In this situation, the teacher typically shows the visitor around the room and tells the visitor what is going on at that time. Why not have students take on this responsibility? After the first few weeks of school, have students brainstorm as a group about what they think are the highlights of their classroom. Then have students role-play, giving each other tours of the room while telling about these highlights. Then, on a rotating basis, students should have the responsibility of actually showing visitors around the room.

Another way to increase students' responsibility as well as communication skills is to have them deliver the announcements at the end of the school day. If you teach elementary school, the announcements will be told before your whole class and will include specific reminders (e.g., "Everyone be sure to take home your math book to study for tomorrow's test," or "Tomorrow is the last day to bring in your permission slip for the circus field trip."). If you teach junior or senior high school, students can deliver announcements over the intercom to the whole school.

Other classroom responsibilities should also be given to students. For example, have students deliver messages to the office secretary, principal, or other teachers. *Don't* have the message written out, but rather require students to deliver the messages orally. Also have students do chores such as taking attendance or collecting lunch money. They'll be forced to communicate actively and effectively in these situations.

One final way to increase students' responsibility and, as a result, their listening and speaking skills is to have them work frequently in small groups. Rather than you leading a classroom discussion in which only one person can speak at a time, give students the topic to discuss and then break them into small groups to discuss the assigned topic. In this situation many more students will be participating as active listeners and speakers.

Times to Develop Listening and Speaking

There are probably some times during your school day that are better than others for developing listening and speaking skills. For example, when students first enter the classroom and are settling down, you might try a "listening and speaking sponge" for a minute or two (e.g., "Find a partner and together think of as many questions as possible that would have the answer *telephone*," or "Find a partner. One of you should pretend to be a seashell, and the other one should pretend to be the ocean. Carry on a conversation for one minute.").

Other prime times to develop students' listening and speaking skills might be Friday afternoons or the afternoons before a school vacation or holiday. During these times, students (and sometimes the teacher) have already mentally started the weekend, holiday, or vacation. Hard-core academic subjects may not be the best topic for these times; instead you might devote the time to listening and speaking activities such as the ones listed below:

1. *Interviewing an Animal* (Plourde 1985, p. 284). You will need slips of paper with animal names written on them. One at a time students select a paper with the name of an animal on it. That student stands in front of the class and is interviewed by the other students. The class must try to guess from the answers to their questions what kind of animal the selected student is. After they guess, another student has a turn.

Sample questions:

- What is a typical day like for you?
- What's your favorite food?
- Where do you sleep?
- Who are your friends?
- How do you move?
- What color are you?
- What are you scared of?
- Who do you scare?
- How fast do you move?

Possible animals:

anteater	ox	skunk	gopher	moose
bumblebee	lion	rhinoceros	worm	seal
gerbil	whale	wolf	giraffe	ant

2. *Campfire Stories* (Plourde 1985, p. 339). You will need a flashlight for this activity. Explain to students that you are going to sit around a pretend campfire and tell stories. Then turn off the lights, pull down the shades, and sit around the flashlight. You might start with a story and then give others a turn. Give students a topic such as "The most exciting thing that ever happened to me," or "My saddest time," or "My funniest time."

3. *Say It Another Way* (Plourde 1988, p. 35). Tell students that it's boring to always say things the same way—that we should try to think of a different way to say things. Divide students into groups of three or four. Give each group a word, such as *eat*, and have them list as many words as they can think of that also mean eat (e.g., *munch, nibble, chew, devour, crunch*). See which group can generate the longest list. Then have each group select two of their words to act out for the other students to guess.

Possible words:

drink	walk	cook	sleep
sit	lie down	see	clean
talk	touch	stand	wash

4. *Penny Patterns* (Plourde 1988, p. 78). Give each student five to ten pennies, depending on how many you have. You should have pennies, too, and sit at a desk in back of the class. Arrange your pennies in a specific pattern on the desk and then tell students how to arrange their pennies so that they look like yours.

For example, you might say, "Put a penny in the center of your desk so that it is head-side up. Next put a penny on the left side of the first penny so that its tail side is up and it is touching the first penny. Then put a penny so that it is diagonally down to the left of the second penny; it must touch the second penny and be head-side up." Continue with several more directions; then have students check to see how they did (you can draw the pattern on the board for them to check). Continue with new patterns as time permits and allow students to give some directions.

5. *Historical-Hysterical Stories* (Plourde 1988, p. 164). Write the names of famous people on slips of paper. Divide students into pairs. Each student selects a paper and then the pairs carry on a conversation as if they really were those famous people. You might have George Washington talking to Michael Jackson or Joan of Arc talking to Cleopatra. The pairs may present their conversations before the class as time permits.

Possible famous people:

George Washington	Joan of Arc
Mickey Mouse	Roy Rogers
Ronald McDonald	Christopher Columbus
Benjamin Franklin	Captain Kangaroo
Abraham Lincoln	Cleopatra
Boy George	John Glenn
Betsy Ross	Babe Ruth
Amelia Earhart	Madonna
Michael Jackson	Cupid
Ronald Reagan	Donald Duck
Mr. Rogers	Jimmy Carter
Zorro	Wizard of Oz

Places to Develop Listening and Speaking Skills

Besides special times to devote to listening and speaking, there are also special places where you can promote listening and speaking in your classroom. For example, you might set up a conversation corner in your classroom—a comfortable place (e.g., two bean-bag chairs, pillows on a carpeted section of the floor, a loft above the coat racks) where students can go when they are finished with their work to quietly converse with each other. Students might talk about what they wish or you might suggest a topic for the day (e.g., "the scariest thing that ever happened to me," "the first job I ever had"). For more ideas on how to set up a conversation corner, see the article "Getting Kids to be Better Communicators" in the July/August issue of *Learning 1986*.

Another place in the classroom to develop listening and speaking skills is at learning centers. You can set up centers where students use a tape recorder to listen to a story or tell their own story. Centers might also have things for two students to do together. For example, a center might have a picture. One student looks at the picture and describes the picture to the other student, who listens carefully and tries to draw a picture that looks just like the one described. A center for older students might have a written job description (e.g., custodian at a large mill, press secretary to the governor) that two students would need to role-play the job interview for, with one being the employer and one the aspiring employee.

A bus ride for a field trip affords another opportunity to develop listening and speaking skills. You might challenge students to jointly name as many items in a given category as possible (e.g., cereals, brands of sneakers, authors whose names start with "S"). Or, using road maps, students can tell partners the exact directions for getting from your school to the location of the field trip.

But wherever you want, whenever you want, however you want—there are many ways to weave in listening and speaking activities throughout the school day. Every one of these ideas will help students to become better listeners and better speakers. Try them!

References

Plourde, Lynn. 1985. *Classroom Listening and Speaking K–2*. Tucson, Ariz.: Communication Skill Builders.

———. "Getting Kids to be Better Communicators." *Learning 86*, July/August 1986, pp. 46–47.

———. 1988. *Classroom Listening and Speaking 3–4*. Tucson, Ariz.: Communication Skill Builders.

22 The Interview Connection

Dene Kay Thomas
University of Idaho

Students in freshman composition come into class as conversationalists, knowing how to use the spoken language in informal situations, especially one-on-one. They visit with each other before class just fine, thank you, and they are quite able to explain why they will have to miss class on Friday or why their paper will have to be a little late. But they have difficulty—in varying degrees—as they attempt to make the transition to formal speaking situations and to writing. Interviews provide two kinds of connections: (1) they are a good middle ground between informal conversation and formal speaking situations, and (2) writing based on an interview lets students use speaking and listening skills to develop their writing skills. In keeping with the belief of learning theorist Jerome Bruner (1966) that learning begins with the familiar and moves on only after making connection with the known, interviews allow students to use the speaking, listening, and writing abilities they already have as they develop new abilities.

I begin by giving the writing assignment for the interview so that students will know what the preparation and practice that lead up to it are for.

Interview Assignment

Interview someone who would be a good subject for a human-interest story or who holds a position that you would like to have in five or ten years. For the human-interest story, here are some guidelines:

Lifestyle

Hobbies

Places Visited

Accomplishments

For the position you would like to hold, analyze what the job entails and what skills are necessary for that position. Here are some guidelines:

Background/Knowledge Needed

Speaking—Formal, Informal

Writing—Within the Company, Outside the Company

Typical Day/Seasonal Variations

Amount of Interaction with People—Customers, Employees, Supervisors

Write up the interview, telling the person's story or informing class members about the position. Entertain class members or help them to decide whether the position would be a good one for them. Hand in two copies of the paper, one for me to grade and one to be circulated for class members to read.

Preparation for the Interview (One Class Day)

As much as possible, I move inductively through the preparation. I start with the overly basic question "What do you need to do an interview?" A list of typical responses looks like this:

paper

pencil

questions

someone to interview

tape recorder (Here we discuss pros and cons.)

Then I say, "OK. I have paper and pencil, and I just happen to have a list of questions here. Who is going to volunteer to let me interview you?" My questions model a bad interview. They are short, they are unconnected, and they require mostly yes-no answers. A sample list:

Where were you born?

How old are you?

Are you married?

Did you vote in the last election?

Do you know very much about nuclear physics?

What's your dog's name?

We go through my list of questions very quickly. Then I ask what went wrong. After all, I had everything that was on our list of what we needed to do an interview. I even had my questions written down. The students tell me problems:

I couldn't tell what you were getting at.

You didn't give her a chance to explain.

The questions were bad.

After a general discussion of what went wrong, I hand out a list of my questions and we analyze them, coming up with categories for questions. The terms may vary, but we usually end up with the following categories:

fact-feeling

open-closed

general-specific

We then talk about questioning strategies and purposes for interviews. An informational interview will include more fact questions, while an interview to find out someone's opinion will include more feeling questions. A specific question often needs to build on the background that is laid by a more general question. Follow-up questions such as "Why?" and "How?" work well to open up a closed question.

An interviewer seldom does nothing but ask questions during an interview. What other responses are appropriate? Here I introduce students to paraphrasing, based on Rogerian reflection (Rogers 1961). A response that paraphrases often begins in one of the following ways:

What I hear you saying is . . .

It sounds like . . .

You seem to feel that . . .

So . . .

It seems to me that you . . .

We practice paraphrasing as a class first. Students give me a feeling statement, and I paraphrase it. If students have trouble thinking of a subject, we brainstorm a list of topics on the board:

classes
college life
parking
registration
abortion
the death penalty
leash laws
smoking

Here are some typical statements and paraphrases:

"Registration is a mess. It took me two hours."
"So the registration system here needs some changes."

"English is boring."
"You don't seem to find English very interesting."

"The food in the dorms is lousy."
"You don't seem to think much of the meals here."

"I think smoking is a dirty habit."
"It sounds like you are strongly against smoking."
"Yeah. My mom smokes and I wish she would quit."
"So your mom's smoking really bothers you."
"Sure. She could die from it."

Although I only ask students to make one statement, my paraphrase often elicits another comment, just as paraphrasing is intended to do.

Next we practice paraphrasing in pairs, with one student making statements and the partner paraphrasing. Often students call me over to ask if their response is a paraphrase. After practicing in pairs, we talk about what happened. Some students clarified the original statement; others misunderstood and the person making the statement corrected them. Here we find out the multiple uses of paraphrasing. It can clarify, serve as a check on understanding, and encourage a further response. Paraphrases are invitations to the people being interviewed to elaborate on what they just said.

Practice Interviews (One Class Day)

As a class, we brainstorm possible questions to ask someone during an interview that will lead to a short newspaper-style human-interest story. Students then individually plan a question sequence for doing an interview with a student in class. In pairs, students interview each other and then write up the interview. As a check on mutual understanding, the writer gives the paper to the person who was interviewed. We read and discuss the accuracy of the papers. I have students give an accuracy rating with a number from one to ten. A ten says, "This is perfect. You have the facts and the feelings, and the emphasis on everything is just exactly right." A one says, "This isn't me at all. You must have interviewed someone else." Most students tend to rate the interviews at an eight or a nine, which gives us room to discuss what was presented well and to talk about slight inaccuracies. Where was a direct quotation especially appropriate? Where was a point made clearly? Where are the slight discrepancies? How did they come about—misunderstanding of facts or feelings, some point overemphasized or not explained, lack of clarity? Was something left out that should have been in there?

Interviews

Students are now ready to do the out-of-class interview that will form the basis for the written assignment. The two options come in here: (1) someone who would make a good subject for a human-interest story, and (2) someone holding a job that the student would like to hold in five to ten years. My students have interviewed mayors, professors, newspaper reporters, taxidermists, karate experts, crop dusters, bouncers, and financial aid officers, to name a few. Most of the people whom students have asked to interview have been wonderfully cooperative. Many want to see a copy of the final paper, thus providing students with another audience for their writing. Just advise them to avoid tax accountants from January through April!

We discuss their choices and how to approach the people. *The Business Writer's Handbook* (Brusaw, Alfred, and Oliu 1987) has a helpful section on interviewing that I have used as a basis for suggestions. The students usually call the people to arrange the interview, explaining who they are, what they want to do, and why they chose the person. The interviews usually last from thirty to sixty minutes. We also talk about the importance of scheduling the interview at a time when students can take thirty to sixty minutes after the interview to jot down extra notes. Memory can be very short, and it's hard to take enough notes during the interview without holding up the interview process.

I allow two weeks for students to complete the interview, though many do it right away. As students complete their interviews, they report to the class on how the interviews went. Sometimes students think of questions they wish they had asked, and they call the people for extra information. Sharing successes and problems gives other students a sense of the variety of experiences that one can have while interviewing.

Students write up rough drafts of the interviews and discuss the drafts in small-group writing conferences, as they do with all their papers. They then revise the papers and hand in two copies: one for me to comment on and one to circulate for the other students to read. Since we have shared so much of the planning and preparation all along, students are very interested in the results.

Follow-ups

I use the interview assignment early in the term. Although I don't expect students to master the art of question asking, paraphrasing, or interviewing during this assignment, the introduction to these skills forms the basis for continued work on them throughout the rest of the term.

We continue the focus on question asking with self-reflexive meta-discourse during work on problem solving, analyzing, and evaluating. We talk about the kinds of questions we ask. I push for students' own discovery of Bloom's taxonomy of questions (1956, 1964). Our original categories of fact and feeling questions correspond to Bloom's cognitive and affective domains. Within those categories, Bloom's divisions are as follows:

Cognitive Domain	*Affective Domain*
1. Knowledge	1. Receiving
2. Comprehension	2. Responding
3. Application	3. Valuing
4. Analysis	4. Organization
5. Synthesis	5. Characterization by a value
6. Evaluation	or value complex

I never present Bloom's divisions; I simply use them as background knowledge for our in-class discussions of kinds of questions and what they accomplish.

I use a similar approach with paraphrasing. During class discussions I frequently ask students to paraphrase what another student said. We develop the habit of commenting on our own comments. The oral paraphrasing that we do regularly provides a connection when we work on paraphrasing written texts. Students then simply extend a skill that they have already begun to develop.

Students continue to use short interviews to gather material for other papers, especially research papers. They have gained an awareness of the interview as an important research tool. They have developed and used connections among speaking, listening, and writing. And they have been involved in active, experiential learning.

Bibliography

Bloom, B. S. 1956. *Taxonomy of Educational Objectives, Handbook I: Cognitive Domain.* New York: McKay.

————. 1964. *Taxonomy of Educational Objectives, Handbook II: Affective Domain.* New York: McKay.

Bruner, J. 1966. *Toward a Theory of Instruction.* Cambridge, Mass.: Harvard University Press.

Brusaw, C. T., G. J. Alfred, and W. E. Oliu. 1987. *The Business Writer's Handbook.* Third edition. New York: St. Martin's Press.

Hunkins, F. P. 1976. *Involving Students in Questioning.* Boston: Allyn and Bacon.

Rogers, C. R. 1961. *Client-Centered Therapy.* Boston: Houghton Mifflin.

23 Listening to the Songs People Sing: Writing Essays Based on Interviews

Deborah DeZure
Eastern Michigan University

Who among us has not felt insecure about understanding others when they speak? We hear the words. We may note the body language and expression. We may even sense what goes unsaid, cleverly hidden in silences, quips, and diversions. But to hear the message behind the words, truly to hear the songs that individual people sing, requires skill and patience in listening, in questioning, and in interpreting.

Buoyed by the belief that these skills can be taught, and convinced that students genuinely want to learn them, I conceived the following assignment for my college composition class:

> Write an essay based on one or more interviews you conduct with an individual on a specific topic. The topic, pre-selected by you and the interviewee, should relate to a controversial or sensitive subject. The essay, 2–3 pages in length, must synthesize the material, using paraphrase and direct quotes where appropriate to support your thesis. Focus on one or more of the recurrent themes presented by the speaker (his/her song). The paper should not be an attempt to recapitulate all the speaker said during the interview, nor should it rely solely on the unedited quotes of the speaker. The paper should present a coherent interpretation of a significant aspect of the interview.

Mild panic ensued among the students, many of whom were from nonverbal homes where communication is primarily (if not solely) functional rather than expressive, and for whom the thought of speaking to an adult is threatening. I immediately gave assurances that we would work on all the necessary skills together, and I introduced concrete approaches to the tasks before them. From the beginning, their fear was mixed with profound gratitude and eagerness to learn skills germane to their personal lives.

The curriculum comprised sets of skills which were introduced by informal lecture-demonstrations, by asking students to practice the skills in class, and by analyzing written examples of interviews and

131

essays based on interviews. Approximately 50 percent of the class time was devoted to conducting interviews, beginning with a class interview of me, interviews of students by their classmates, and a class interview of a guest speaker. Each of these was followed by analysis and discussion of the interview process.

Selecting an Interview Topic and Interviewee

Since the students' final written products would be only as good as their raw material, I advised them to select a topic which was likely to render compelling material for them to develop. To ensure the power of that material, I built controversy and/or sensitivity into the requirements for the interview topic. Experienced writers and interviewers may be able to make the most mundane material interesting. For beginners, however, selecting provocative subjects gave them an opportunity to elicit stronger raw material and the challenge of dealing with difficult interpersonal issues as listeners and questioners.

I suggested the following topics:

1. A person's beliefs or attitudes about a specific subject on which the speaker is well-versed, e.g., a genetic engineer speaking on gene splicing.

2. A period in a person's life, e.g., immigration experiences.

3. The impact of a unique characteristic on a person's total life experience, e.g., minority status, life as a twin, coping with illness.

4. A unique hobby or commitment pursued with a passion, such as working for an organization, e.g., MADD or a political party.

5. A critical incident or life event, e.g., childbirth, a reunion.

6. A person's career and his/her feelings about it. Focus on fulfillment and lifestyle rather than a straightforward job description.

I urged students to take chances, to push themselves to talk with people and about topics which they had avoided in the past. If their initial interviewee was not responsive, or if the topic proved to be limited, I encouraged them to modify the topic or find a new interviewee and begin the process again.

A sampling of topics selected by my undergraduates included interviews with the following: a rape victim, a quadriplegic, a Vietnam veteran, a mayor, a grandparent describing life in 1910, and a college athlete who had accepted payoffs discussing fraud in college athletics. Despite my offer to help find interviewees, all students found speakers on their own.

These topics did render powerful essays. Although many interviewees enjoyed the interview experience, I discussed with students the ethics of "using" the experience of another person's pain for personal, albeit academic, goals. This issue gained special meaning for students when the class interviewed a survivor of the Auschwitz concentration camp, who, despite her desire to share her experiences with a generation of students who knew little of the Holocaust, clearly was in pain as she recalled those experiences.

Students were instructed to explain to their interviewee that the interview was a class assignment; to discuss the parameters of the topic, including areas the speaker might wish to omit; and to decide beginning and ending times for each session, a location, and a method of recording the session. Use of a tape or video recorder was optional but could be employed with the interviewee's consent. Even if a tape recorder was used, students were to take notes on visual cues, their immediate impressions of body language and expression, and inquiries to return to later in the interview. Students prepared numerous interview questions representing general, specific, open-ended, and closed inquiries with rankings to indicate their priorities. Finally, I suggested that students thank their interviewees formally when the interview was concluded.

Processes as Content

Using lecture-demonstrations, I introduced several processes and concepts. Students applied them repeatedly while preparing and conducting interviews and analyzing both live interviews and transcripts.

In two class periods, I provided the following guidelines:

Setting the Stage

The primary goal in an interview is to create a climate in which other people can and will reveal themselves to you. Help interviewees tell their stories by facilitating their ability to remember, reflect, analyze, clarify, and describe their feelings, insights, and attitudes.

Listening

1. Be an active listener. Show interest. Look at the speaker. Use your body language to show your involvement and indicate that you are continuously alert and responsive to what is being said.

2. Show empathy and support. When the interviewee speaks of difficult or sad topics, for example, indicate with facial expressions or gentle comments that you understand it is difficult for the speaker to share these thoughts, but you are prepared to hear them.

Be sensitive to the needs of the speaker. You are not a journalist in need of a hot scoop. If the speaker is uncomfortable, consider changing or redirecting a line of inquiry, or give that option to the speaker. A helpful comment is "I see that this topic makes you uncomfortable. Would you like to move on to another topic or take a little break?" Providing support reassures the speaker that someone is truly listening.

Some of what you hear may be painful and make you feel anxious because you cannot ameliorate the speaker's problems. Most people do not expect you to solve their problems. They are grateful to have someone listen with care.

3. Be patient. Give the speaker time to reflect and to speak. Resist the urge to fill every quiet moment with talk. First thoughts are not always the most valid indicators of feelings. Giving a speaker extra time to think is time well-spent. The speaker may use that time to connect to relevant memories and initiate areas of discussion you could not have anticipated. Don't be afraid of silence. Let it work for you.

Time is especially important with the elderly. Many older people need more time to process information, to collect their thoughts, and to articulate their answers. If they sense your impatience, they will cut short their answers and feel frustrated that they have not conveyed their views.

4. Provide cues to help the speaker develop ideas. Cues also indicate that you are listening and you desire to hear more about a topic. Helpful cues include "Can you tell me more about that?" "Can you give me an example of that?" "How do you feel about that?" "How did that make you feel?"

5. Periodically repeat or rephrase what the speaker has said to verify that you have understood. For example, "In other words, you feel that X led to Y. Have I understood you correctly?"

6. Do not impose your views on the interview. It is not a debate, nor is it necessary for the speaker to understand your position at this

time. Even if you disagree with the speaker, do not be confrontational or aggressive. The speaker will feel defensive, and the level of trust will plummet. If you wish clarification on an issue, especially when you disagree, use such facilitative comments as "Could you help me understand your position on this?" or "Could you help me to understand how you arrived at your views?"

Questioning

1. The questions we ask determine the nature and scope of the answers we derive (Langer 1973). This concept needs to be emphasized in all stages of the interview process, from preparing questions to interpreting answers.

2. There are many useful taxonomies of questions. For this assignment, however, understanding the distinctions between *general* and *specific, abstract* and *concrete,* and *open-ended* and *closed* inquiries is facilitative and sufficient.

3. Avoid "loaded" questions which imply an answer or limit the speaker's response. For example, "What contributes to your unhappiness at work?" is loaded unless the speaker has indicated his/her discontent.

4. Discussion is usually more restrained and awkward early in the interview. Return to questions later in the interview if you feel the original answer was unclear, evasive, or not addressed. Rephrase the question or use material you learn during the interview to stimulate the speaker's recall.

5. Beware of sexism, racism, and bias in your assumptions and your language.

6. Periodically give the speaker a chance to comment freely and to initiate discussion topics. Helpful questions include "Is there anything you want to say about this topic which we haven't discussed?" or "Is there anything you would like to add or modify about what you have said thus far?" These questions invite the speaker to correct omissions and allow him/her to feel more in control.

In-Class Interviews

Immediately following a lecture-demonstration of the above concepts, we began in-class interviews. Students interviewed me on "Living in New York City." I chose this topic because I am a former New Yorker now living and teaching in a small midwestern city where students tend to be curious about life in the Big Apple. Their initial efforts at interviewing gave us ample material to see the dynamics of interview technique at work:

> *Student 1:* How many times were you mugged in New York City?
> *Professor:* Never. [Silence]
> *Student 2:* What were your favorite things to do in New York?
> *Professor:* Spend time with my family, go to museums and theatre.
> *Student 2:* [No follow-up]
> *Student 3:* How did you feel about living in New York?
> *Professor:* I loved it. I . . . [a three-minute oration followed].

At this point I stopped the interview so we could reflect on what had just occurred. Students could readily see that beginning the interview with such a specific, closed question brought them virtually no valuable information and led nowhere. They also recognized the assumptions about New York City inherent in the question. The inquiry about favorite activities was effective because it elicited specific information. However, it was limited without a follow-up for clarification, e.g., "Why?" or "Can you tell us more about them?" In contrast, the open-ended inquiry, "How did you feel about living in New York City?" was just the opportunity to reveal my feelings.

But not all interviewees do well with such general inquiries, as was demonstrated in the next interview. A male student (Bob) interviewed a female student (Ann) in front of the class where everyone could observe their interaction on the topic "What will your life be like ten years from now?"

> *Bob:* What will your life be like ten years from now?
> *Ann:* [Long silence] Well, in what way?
> *Bob:* What will your career be?
> *Ann:* I'll be a marine biologist and probably live near an ocean.
> *Bob:* And how many children will you have?
> *Ann:* [Silence . . . grimace] What makes you think I'll have children or be married—just because I'm a female? I'm the oldest of nine children and I have no plans to have kids.

Again, it did not take long to generate material to analyze in class. Students quickly realized that the generality of a question affects the speaker's ability to respond. The first question, a restatement of the topic, was far too general and abstract. The question about her career was useful, but without a follow-up, Bob lost a lot of material in his haste to pursue the next line of inquiry. And finally, his assumption that Ann would have children made her, and other women students, angry. Bob later acknowledged that his question was sexist because he would not have asked it of a male.

Students then paired off and interviewed each other on the same topic. We later reconvened to discuss their problems and insights into the interviewing process. The following guidelines were provided for interpreting interview data:

Interpreting

Begin with your gut feelings and challenge your tentative conclusions by asking yourself the following questions:

1. What is my overall sense of what was truly important to the speaker?
   A. Which topics were emphasized by repetition and which were omitted, evaded, or undeveloped?
   B. Which topics did the speaker take extra time to develop using great detail, emotive language, and emphatic voice inflection and expression?

2. What visual clues can aid in interpretation? Did the speaker's physical appearance, posture, body language, and facial expressions indicate attitudes and feelings?

3. Was there congruence between what the speaker said and how the speaker said it? If not, what might explain the disparity? In the speaker's comments, what was fact and what was feeling, and which facts were particularly influenced by feelings?

4. Were there any comments or incidents before or after the interview—for example, in the selection of an interview topic which might help me to interpret the interview material?

Choosing and Supporting a Thesis

Interpreting an interview is a complex and intimidating task for students. I encouraged them to reject the impulse to tie everything together in a neat package. Instead, I suggested that they pull out a few dominant threads from the speaker's comments, attempt to develop each, and select the one which renders the most interesting and well-supported thesis. Interviews tend to be sprawling with many unrelated or undeveloped elements, adding confusion to an already difficult task.

I used two methods to demonstrate this crucial selection process. Students read excerpts from Studs Terkel's *Working* (1972), in which individuals discuss their lives and work. I then asked students to find three themes they could develop for each excerpt. As a class, we listed their themes, demonstrating that many topics are possible from any one interview.

The second method was analysis of a dramatic presentation by a guest speaker. A survivor of Auschwitz described her experiences. Students had generated and discussed interview questions, which I had given to the speaker before the presentation. Because she was retelling a period in her life which had an organic unity of its own, she preferred to describe it as a continuous narrative, incorporating responses to their questions. It was informative, engrossing, enraging, and poignant. At the next class, we discussed students' personal reactions to the experience of listening to such harsh and shocking events from this soft-spoken woman. Students felt shock at "witnessing" the result of humankind's potential for inhumanity and yet felt pride at their ability to cope with listening to and empathizing with her pain. Many felt that there was nothing they would be afraid to hear in the future. We then began to interpret what we heard and saw and to identify themes which could be developed for an essay.

We concluded the unit with an analysis of essays based on interviews. In keeping with the emphasis on topics requiring sensitivity or controversy, we discussed compelling essays describing the feelings of a man dying from AIDS (Morrisroe 1985) and the experiences of Japanese Americans interned in the United States during World War II (Kirk 1985).

The Interview Essays

When the first drafts of the students' interview essays were completed, peer evaluation based on specific criteria was used. The strongest essay in each evaluation group was read to the class. Paper after paper was powerful and moving. These students had learned their lessons well. They had questioned and listened. They had taken chances and permitted themselves to feel for others and empathize with them. They had heard unique and gripping tales, and many had understood the songs of sadness and pride, confusion and hope— the songs of human beings who want and deserve to be heard. But what I, as their teacher, sensed beyond their efforts to write sensitive and insightful essays was a new confidence and willingness to share feelings and thoughts—to elicit truly personal revelations, to listen with care, and to be heard.

References

Kirk, Veronica. 1985. The Internment of Japanese Americans. *Ann Arbor News*, December 4, 1985, pp. E1, E2.

Langer, Suzanne. 1973. *Philosophy in a New Key: A Study of the Symbolism of Reason, Rite, and Art.* Cambridge, Mass.: Harvard University Press.

Morrisroe, Patricia. 1985. AIDS: One Man's Story. *New York* 18 (August 19, 1985): 28–35.

Terkel, Studs. 1972. *Working: People Talk about What They Do All Day and How They Feel about What They Do.* New York: Pantheon Books.

24 Positive Strokes: An Affective Oral Language Activity

Annis L. Cassells
Curran Junior High
Bakersfield, California

Junior high students are notorious for their tough and crude exteriors, their I-don't-care attitudes, and their flippant responses or, conversely, non-responses. However, on Positive Strokes days they prove this stereotype to be in error. On these days an observer would hear genuine complimentary comments, see active listening, and sense the pervading atmosphere of caring and camaraderie. He or she would witness the gamut of emotions and the shedding of numerous tears— by students and teacher—not at all what one might expect in a junior high school classroom.

Positive Strokes is one of those ideas that comes to teachers in a flash of enlightenment after finishing up the roll and looking out into those June-blues faces that are just marking time until graduation day. It came to me near the end of my first year of teaching in the GATE (Gifted And Talented Education) program. Acquainting myself with gifted youngsters and doing nightly stints at my desk to meet their varied needs, talents, and abilities was quite a challenge. Add the dimension of riding herd on a fairly tough, out-of-hand group of eighth graders, and you would have found one rather frazzled teacher standing at the podium that day. Then the light bulb of Positive Strokes glowed in my head.

I told the class that this would be their opportunity to say something good or nice to anyone in the class—only positive comments would be acceptable. Anyone who cared to speak would speak directly to the classmate being addressed, and the rest of us would listen without comment. "The purpose?" they quizzed. "To give everyone the opportunity to say something nice to another member of the class. Perhaps you may have *thought* this comment before but never had the chance to say it aloud. Remember, it won't be long until we're never together in this total group again," I answered, still feeling the

140

glow, regardless of their rather apprehensive and self-conscious looks. These kids were masters of the verbal putdown, but this new positive thing called for digging into previously untapped resources within themselves.

I chose the first student that we would compliment, taking care to select someone who was well-liked. "Positive comments for Rosemary?" I cheerfully boomed. Then I waited.

Some dear little soul spoke up: "You're always nice to people, and everybody likes you." The look of surprise on Rosemary's face was priceless.

Then another brave person said, "Thanks for the help you gave me in math this year."

If there was a lull, I'd ask, "Are there more positive comments for Rosemary?" When it was apparent that there weren't, it was my turn to say something positive to her. I praised her development as a writer, her kindness to others, and her maturity. Then there were two of us glowing.

Rosemary chose the next person and made the first comment about him. Then we proceeded as before. The students were beginning to get involved.

All was going fairly well when Allan, who was of superior intelligence but had not laid to rest a previous battle, picked John, his archenemy and class oddball, to be complimented next. We all knew that Allan's choice had been out of meanness; their latest altercation was fresh in all our minds. John poked out his chin in readiness for the verbal blows he expected, and Allan let fly with a comment that held a double meaning. However, before the air was silent, Lisa spoke up and told of the great improvement that John had made since the beginning of the year. Other students spoke up if they could find even the tiniest positive thing to say. John's strained and defiant face became relaxed and hopeful. I felt the tears welling up in my eyes and spilling down onto my cheeks.

That first two-day Positive Strokes session was memorable. We all learned about the power of language and the power of positive peer regard to lift self-esteem. We learned that people often brace themselves for scathing words but have difficulty accepting compliments and that we need to be able to accept the nice things that others say to us.

A pleasant and touching sideline of this exercise was the class's decision to give positive strokes to me. I discovered that I needed a lot of practice in accepting praise, too. The class beamed and kept handing me Kleenex.

Since that first time four years ago, Positive Strokes has become a standard end-of-the-year activity. The eighth graders remind me that I'd better make time for it because the school year is running out. Of course the seventh graders wonder what it's all about. They look rather skeptical at first, but they soon join in.

It was with great pride this past June that I observed exchanges such as these:

"You're just a great girl, and you've been someone I could count on this year when I was feeling down."

"You were the first one to speak to me when I came new into this class."

"I know we've laughed at you and your car designs, but I really do think they're good and someday you're gonna be famous."

"I'm glad I met you this year, and I hope to get to know you better next year."

"I'm sorry for the way I treated you at the beginning of the year, and I'm glad we got to be friends."

"You've been such a friend to me from the first day of junior high. You're my best friend, and I'll miss you so much next year when we're at different high schools."

"I love to hear you laugh and the way you say, 'Oh, no!' "

"Remember when we had that journal assignment where we had to recommend someone for the outstanding student award? Well, I picked you because you always try hard and do your best and get just about perfect on everything."

"People tease you a lot about being Chinese, but you never get mad. You just shine 'em on."

"When we had study groups you got right to work on those definitions and shared what you had with me. I appreciated that."

"I admire the way you're always smiling."

This oral language activity is more than an exercise that promotes speaking and listening skills. It has the power to get inside each student and touch his or her emotions. A bonding occurs during this time of shared emotional expression that helps transform a classroom of individualists into a cohesive unit. This fact makes a strong case for using the Positive Strokes activity more frequently than at the end of the year.

Comments that are meant for another seem to have an impact on each listener. Receiving affirmation from their peers and hearing what constitutes desirable and valued behavior is especially crucial for adolescents; it plays a major role in helping them to sort out the jigsaw pieces of their own identities.

Positive Strokes also allows me to publicly communicate special messages to individual students, with implications for all. I told one student that I had observed her strength of character in the face of defeat several times this year. I had seen her *not* give up. I explained that this was the type of strength that people needed to survive throughout life and that she had already demonstrated that she had that strength. Apparently, my statement stayed on her mind because a few days later she reminded me of it and asked me if I had meant it. Another student, who had accomplished little this year, and his classmates heard me say that I felt that he'd been in a "holding pattern" this year but that I was confident that he would come out of it and that he had the ability to succeed in whatever he chose.

The boost in self-esteem and the opportunity to practice social skills that will help ensure success in getting along in our world today and tomorrow are further attributes of Positive Strokes. A seventh grader this year told me that he had really become more open and able to say things that he never thought he could before. He felt good about his accomplishment. I felt pretty terrific, myself. Please pass the Kleenex.

Editor

Patricia Phelan is chair of the Classroom Practices Committee of NCTE. She is currently a teacher-leader in the California Literature Project, a Mentor teacher, and English Department chair at University City High School in San Diego. A fellow in the San Diego Area Writing Project and the Humanities Institute, she has degrees in political science, English, and education. She has written curriculum for her school district, contributed to a language arts textbook, and published in *English Journal* and NCTE affiliate journals.

Titles in the Classroom Practices in Teaching English Series

NCTE began publishing the Classroom Practices series in 1963 with *Promising Practices in the Teaching of English*. Volumes 1–16 of the series are out of print. The following titles are available through the NCTE *Catalog*.